Two week loan

Please return on or before the last date stamped below.
Charges are made for late return.

IS 239/0799

INFORMATION SERVICES PO BOX 430, CARDIFF CF10 3XT

First published 1988
by
Beyond the Pale Publications
7 Winetavern Street,
Belfast BT1 1JQ

ISBN 0 9514229 0 1 (pbk)

This publication is available from
Obair,
Conway Mill,
Conway Street,
Belfast.
Tel. 238353

Printed by:
Express Litho Ltd.,
Belfast
Typeset at Oxford University Computing Service

Contents

List of Illustrations

Figures

Tables

Foreword by *Obair* Committee

Obair: The Campaign for Employment in West Belfast was established in 1987. It came about as the result of discussions among a number of individuals who had been involved in various community and employment creation projects in West Belfast. They had been brought together on the initiative of the Member of Parliament for the area, Gerry Adams, to discuss the chronic unemployment which has affected West Belfast for years. Out of the discussions the *Obair* campaign was born. *Obair* is a Gaelige word, the English equivalent of which is 'work'.

It was agreed that *Obair* would be an open campaign. Thus it is non-party political and non-sectarian, seeking support from anyone who accepts the *Obair* aims and objectives. These are enshrined in a basic 'Charter of Employment Rights' which were endorsed at a public meeting on 2nd May 1988 in West Belfast, to which all political parties, religious leaders, community and employment projects, and trade unions were invited. The meeting took into account the community divisions in West Belfast and noted the unemployment difficulties throughout this area.

Thus the *Obair* charter enshrines the basic principle that everyone has the right to meaningful, properly paid employment and that discrimination on any grounds is unacceptable. The charter also declares as unacceptable the situation where a large section of the population is subjected to long term mass unemployment. A campaign to internationalise and win support for the *Obair* charter was initiated and is continuing.

In the course of this campaign *Obair* came to appreciate more fully the sterling work done by the MacBride principles campaign. *Obair* supports the MacBride principles and commends those who have worked in support of their basic and modest measures.

A Review of the Unemployment Problem

It quickly became clear to the group in its initial discussions, that before any serious attempt could be made to address the unemployment crisis in West Belfast a clear understanding of the nature and causes of the problem was necessary. Just as quickly we discovered that those statutory bodies, whose responsibility it is to provide the basic information on the subject, had consistently failed to do so. The next step therefore was to address this absence of in-depth information on the history of, and background to, the unemployment situation in this area. A study was commissioned to assess the extent of the problem and reveal its causes. This task was taken on by Dr Bill Rolston, University of Ulster, and Mike Tomlinson, Queen's University, assisted by Geraldine McAteer. *Obair* thanks them. The result of their collective efforts is the following report. We note, with considerable pride, that this is the first such report to be compiled on the unemployment problems of West Belfast. It is an indictment of those charged with this responsibility with all their resources that such a report was not commissioned by them but by those whose interests they purport to represent.

Causes of the Problem

Obair believes that this report illustrates that the chronic levels of unemployment that we suffer have not come about accidentally. They are not the result, as some have tried to suggest, of a work-shy community. Nor, indeed, are they the result of a policy on the part of any section of our community to deliberately create unemployment in the area in an attempt to foment discontent. The reality, as outlined in this report, is that massive levels of unemployment have been a characteristic of West Belfast long before the present level of political instability came about. Unemployment in this area has two main causes;

1. A history of neglect by successive unionist and British administrations.
2. Continued discrimination in the allocation of finance, the location of industry and the development of the economic infrastructure.

The report, in our opinion, underlines very clearly, in both its content and conclusions, the existence of a system of ingrained structural discrimination which is practised against areas such as West Belfast with devastating economic, social and human effects.

Proposals

The report also makes a number of proposals which form, we believe, the basis for a programme to resolve these major problems. The launching of this report marks a new phase in the *Obair* campaign. It will become a central part of an international effort aimed at highlighting the unemployment crisis in West Belfast. It will be the spearhead of an education and information offensive to place the chronic unemployment situation in this area at the centre of a political debate which will build national and international pressure on the British Government to resolve the problem. *Obair* is committed to supporting and encouraging all genuine attempts to create real and meaningful employment in West Belfast. The contents of this report represent a challenge to the British government to initiate a major programme of development under the control and direction of the people of West Belfast.

The adoption of the proposals contained in this report provide the basis for such a programme. These proposals could begin to reverse the decades of discrimination and neglect which have been inflicted upon the people of West Belfast.

We trust that its contents will be studied by those in power. We are confident that it will be welcomed by the people of West Belfast. This report is dedicated to them and to the future.

OBAIR

CAMPAIGN FOR EMPLOYMENT IN WEST BELFAST

Campaign Charter

Access to meaningful, properly paid employment is a basic human right.

Forced unemployment is a gross injustice against those who have to endure it. It is a shameful waste of human talent and resources.

Equality of opportunity in employment is also a basic human right.

Discrimination in employment, whether individually or structurally directed, is a violation of this basic human right.

Long term mass unemployment, where a large section of the population suffers forced unemployment for periods of years, amounts to a sustained assault on the rights of those affected.

The burdens of lower living standards and the stunting of expectations are compounded by a mass of social problems which invariably spring up in such a situation.

In West Belfast we have experienced unemployment at levels, and for durations which are totally and utterly unacceptable. In parts of the areas unemployment levels between 80% and 90% have existed, not only for years but indeed, for decades.

Given the seriousness of the situation we have decided to launch a campaign to highlight and help rectify the unemployment crisis in West Belfast.

Campaign Aims

The aims of the campaign are as follows:
1. To end unemployment in West Belfast.
2. To end discrimination in employment in West Belfast.

OBAIR

CAMPAIGN FOR EMPLOYMENT IN WEST BELFAST

OBAIR: The Campaign for Employment in West Belfast, is a non-party political. non-sectarian, community based campaign.

The OBAIR charter, and the aims of the campaign have received support from a wide spectrum of groups and individuals, and were unanimously endorsed at a well attended public meeting in West Belfast in May 1988. In addition, a large number of people and organisations from West Belfast and further afield, have agreed to act as sponsors for the OBAIR campaign. We would like to take this opportunity to express our gratitude for their support. To date the list of sponsors is:

LIST OF SPONSORS

The OBAIR campaign continues to seek the broadest possible support and accordingly we invite all those who agree with the OBAIR charter and aims, to complete the sponsorship form below, and return it to us as soon as possible. The names of sponsors will be used to show the extent of support for the OBAIR initiative.

Gerry Adams, MP, President, Sinn Fein
American Education Committee
William Attley, General Secretary, Federated Workers Union of Ireland
Robert Ballagh, Artist
Ballymurphy People's Theatre
Ballymurphy Tenants's Association
Ballymurphy Tenants' Association Youth Group
Ballymurphy Workingmen's Club
Ciaran De Baroid
Belfast Community Theatre
Belfast Esposed
Tony Benn, MP
Des Bonass, ATGWU
Between
Ronan Brady, Management Secretary, Larkin Unemployed Centre, Dublin
Brid Brennan
Bernard Brown Federated Workers Union of Ireland
Campaign Group of MPs
Ben Carney, ATGWU
Martin Collins, Writer, Editor *Labour and Ireland*
Concerned Community Organiations
Conway Community Enterprises
Jeremy Corbyn, MP
Derry Trades Council
J.G. Devlin, Actor
Charlie Douglas, ATGWU
Falls Community Council
Michael Farrell, Writer
Philip Flynn, General Secretary, LGPSU
Gort Na Mona Parent Youth Support Group
Gort Na Mona Tenants' Association
Noirin Greene, ITGWU Executive, ICTU Executive
Eugene Hickland, Secretary, Irish National Organisation of Unemployed

Horn Drive Drop-in
Information on Ireland
Linton Kwesi Johnston Poet
Michael Kane, Painter, Member of AOSDANA
Oliver Kelly Solicitor
Peter King, Nausau County Comptroller, (USA)
Lenadoon Community Youth Group
Ken Livingstone, MP
Ken Loach, Film-maker
Lower Lenadoon Housing Action Committee
Sean MacAnderson, Editor *Andersonstown News*
Bernadette McAliskey
P.J. McGrory, Solicitor
Alex Maskey, Belfast Councillor
Matt Talbot Youth Club
John Mitchell, General Secretary, IDATU
Moyard Housing Action Group
Naionra Bharr an Chluanai
Ulick O'Connor, Writer
Kevin O'Donnell, Secretary, West Belfast Communist Party
Paul O'Dwyer
Rocklands Environmental Group
Alan Sapper, General Secretary, ACTT
Denis Skinner, MP
Springhill Community House Ltd
Springhill Education Project
Suffolk Adventure Group
Twinbrook Tenants' Association
Upper Springfield Resource Centre
West Belfast Parent Youth Support Group.

Preface

Commissioned by *Obair, the Campaign for Employment in West Belfast,* to examine the extent of unemployment in the constituency, we produced a Report in September 1988. A limited number of copies of this Report were photocopied and spiral-bound. These were then sold at a price beyond the reach of most people in the constituency, especially the unemployed. This book is a slightly revised and up-dated version of the original *Obair* Report. We have produced it for two reasons. Firstly, it is clear that there is a heavy demand for the Report which sold out in a couple of weeks. Secondly, we want to make our findings more accessible to the constituents of West Belfast by producing a publication which they may be able to afford. After all, in the debate within the constituency about economic development, the people of the area have as much right to this information as those in government Departments for whom buying the original Report was no problem.

Bill Rolston
Mike Tomlinson

Belfast
November 1988

Acknowledgements

While putting this report together, we received invaluable assistance and support from an astonishing range of people, some without work, some who work for no pay, others who work for little pay and still others who are paid very well. Help has come from community groups, trade unions, civil servants, other statutory sector workers, private sector employees, a few self-employed people, those involved with voluntary agencies, ACE and YTP workers, and from a number of unemployed people. All of these have provided access to information and experience which we hope the report does justice to. Another group of people contributed to the report's progress by taking over some of our personal responsibilities, including parenting.

Some of the aforementioned would not want to be named, others have said they mustn't be named and there are one or two who might like to be named but aren't going to be. There are some who are completely unaware of their contribution to this report, or do not know just how helpful they have been.

To all these 'participants', conscious or unconscious, reluctant or willing, a big thank you.

We are particularly indebted to Denis O'Hearn for assistance with historical material.

Belfast Exposed responded at very short notice to a request for photographs and we are grateful for permission to publish them in this book.

1.

Introduction

In November 1987 we were invited to a meeting of *Obair, The Campaign for Employment in West Belfast* to discuss drawing up a report on the problems facing the West Belfast area. *Obair* had prepared a charter based on the right to meaningful and properly paid work, and on the right to equality of access to employment. It was hoped that this charter, with its clear statement of principles and human rights, would become the rallying point for a widely supported non-party-political and non-sectarian campaign to promote employment. At that stage, sponsorship for the charter was being sought from a broad range of individuals and groups both within and outside of Ireland.

We were in full sympathy with *Obair's* charter and agreed to act as research consultants to the campaign. Before the end of the year we were given a brief to:

> 'review and discuss the available evidence on the unemployment problem in West Belfast'.

This report is the outcome.

Interim Report

In March 1988 we presented an eight-page interim report to *Obair* in order to indicate the lines of our inquiry and to establish some key points. Although this report was not intended for publication, we were able to use some of its details for the public launch of the campaign on the May Day bank holiday. For instance, almost 10% of all those officially recorded as unemployed in the North of Ireland reside in the parliamentary constituency of West Belfast. Indeed, in some parts of the constituency the *employment* rate was barely above this figure. It was already clear to us that unemployment had plagued the area for decades. Relative to other parts of the Belfast urban area, West Belfast has witnessed a process of disinvestment and job decline which successive governments have failed to reverse. As we stated in the interim report,

> 'notwithstanding the massive obstacles facing the people of West Belfast, great efforts have been made to generate employment with little or no support from the state. These efforts have often been frustrated by the British government or its agencies.'

Political Football

Since we began our research there has been much talk of a government-backed economic initiative for West Belfast. This 'option' has been on the agenda of the Anglo-Irish Conference since the beginning of the year (1988). Calls for a major economic development programme have come from elected representatives belonging to a range of political parties, from priests and bishops, from community groups and, of course, from *Obair* itself. For months there were little more than guarded statements from the Secretary of State. For instance the joint statement issued after the 17 June meeting of the Anglo-Irish Conference reported that,

> 'the Secretary of State said he hoped shortly to make a statement about further measures to improve the performance of the public sector, and stimulate involvement of the private and voluntary sectors, in areas of Belfast characterised by exceptionally high unemployment and poor rates of economic activity. These measures would begin in the current financial year and would involve action to enhance employment opportunities and to improve the conditions of life in these areas.'

In plain language, the government will procede with its planned reductions of services in the fields of education, health, housing and social security, but hopes that private and voluntary agencies can be persuaded to pick up the consequences. Furthermore, the latter agencies can expect to receive additional funding for 'training' and 'special employment measures' (such as the Action for Community Employment scheme), although this funding will not necessarily be targeted on West Belfast alone.

Development Debate

In West Belfast itself, there is widespread agreement that a concerted programme of action on economic and social development is required. The speculation surrounding an initiative from government has, however, stimulated many different ideas on *how* the problems should be tackled. There appears to be disagreement over the volume of resources needed, what to spend the money on, and who to channel initiatives through. Should the Industrial Development Board continue to scour the world in search of footloose investment? Or should economic development be locally-based? Do we need more or less training, and of what kind? Is it time to give up on manufacturing industry and to adopt a service-based strategy? Would co-operatives, including a co-operative bank, provide an appropriate institutional framework for development, or are 'enterprise centres' the thing of the future?[1]

In July, just as we were finalising the contents of this report, the long-awaited aid package was announced. Ten million pounds is to be spread over North and West Belfast in improving roads and street lighting, patching up school buildings, adapting premises for adult education and in furthering the government's idea of economic development through job clubs, enterprise centres and an expansion of existing employment and training schemes. LEDU will also get an additional £500,000 to spend. No matter what the small print of this initiative says, it will not do justice to either the extent of the problems or to the development debate which is now in progress. The amount promised has already been described as 'a drop in the ocean' and as 'tokenism'.[2]

The fact that the development debate is well underway might suggest that our brief for writing this report is redundant. Why review the evidence on unemployment when the facts are well-known? We accept that the focus of discussion should be on solutions rather than endless, repetitious descriptions of problems. At the same time, we believe it is important to discuss why West Belfast contains so much unemployment and attendant social problems. Appropriate solutions can only be constructed if the problem is properly understood. Nevertheless, we have decided to exceed our brief by not only reviewing the arguments over the general direction which economic and social development should take, but also by making a number of specific policy proposals in relation to the private and public sectors of the economy.

Previous Reports

This is not the first report on unemployment in West Belfast, nor will it be the last. In recent years, there have been many attempts to draw attention to unemployment, poverty, absence of child care facilities, ill-health, unacceptable housing conditions, lack of educational facilities, low benefit take-up and other problems.[3] Most of these have been concerned with particular neighbourhoods or housing estates within West Belfast. These reports have proved an essential starting point for our own inquiry. In particular, we have benefited from the work put into the 'Public Inquiry into Unemployment' organised by Springhill Community House in 1983, a wide-ranging inquiry which aired many issues from the social consequences of unemployment to economic strategies.

Government agencies have also provided information which illustrates the extent of unemployment and social deprivation in West Belfast. One of the first official reports to focus attention on the area appeared in 1976. The Belfast Areas of Special Social Need Report[4] (commonly known as 'the BAN Report') mapped each electoral ward of the Belfast urban area using a variety of indicators (such as unemployment rate). This report spoke of two major 'need syndromes':

> 'One is characterised by unemployment, low incomes, and overcrowded housing ... This has a west Belfast distribution. The other is an inner city syndrome, distinguished by substandard housing, poor physical environment, low incomes, lack of skills

and concentrations of persons with different forms of personal handicap whether associated with age or health.'[5]

Evidently parts of West Belfast exemplified both syndromes. Twelve years later, the situation is in most respects far worse than it was, as we shall see. The growth in unemployment is largely responsible.

What is West Belfast?

Since the production of the BAN Report, the Housing Executive has been the only agency to publish comprehensive survey data which allows West Belfast to be compared with other areas.[6] The Executive's presentation of research findings, however, makes it difficult to draw detailed conclusions about changes over time and to compare these results with other data. This is because of lack of agreement within government agencies over the precise geographical definition of West Belfast. To the Housing Executive (and we suspect to many of those living outside the area), West Belfast means 'Catholic West Belfast', an area bounded by 'the peace line' and the M1 motorway, stretching right out to Twinbrook and Poleglass in the Lisburn District Council area; to the Department of Economic Development (DED), West Belfast is the parliamentary constituency, which includes some predominantly Protestant wards; to the Department of Health and Social Services (DHSS), West Belfast is swallowed up in the North and West Belfast Unit of Management; to the RUC, it is 'B' Division; and so on.

For the purposes of this report, West Belfast is taken to mean the streets and neighbourhoods which make up the Westminster parliamentary constituency, unless we indicate otherwise. Two points should be noted with respect to this definition. Firstly, the constituency is not strictly speaking a mere aggregate of Belfast District Council wards as some government departments seem to think. For some reason, the Boundary Commission revises district council areas and UK parliamentary constituency boundaries quite separately and at different times. The current constituency boundary follows the lines of *Belfast District Council wards as they were before they were revised in 1984*. This means that the present constituency boundary cuts through the middle of several of the new district council wards. For instance, the old Shankill ward which used to be outside of the West Belfast constituency is now, in its enlarged and revised form, split between North and West Belfast constituencies. Secondly, as can be seen from the map in Figure 1.1, much of Belfast Lough and the city centre technically fall within the constituency boundary. This would be significant if the 'business vote' remained or indeed if seagulls had votes! But in no meaningful political, economic or social sense does the city centre 'belong' to West Belfast, so we are excluding it from our constituency-based definition. The electoral wards which make up the area are listed in Figure 1.2.

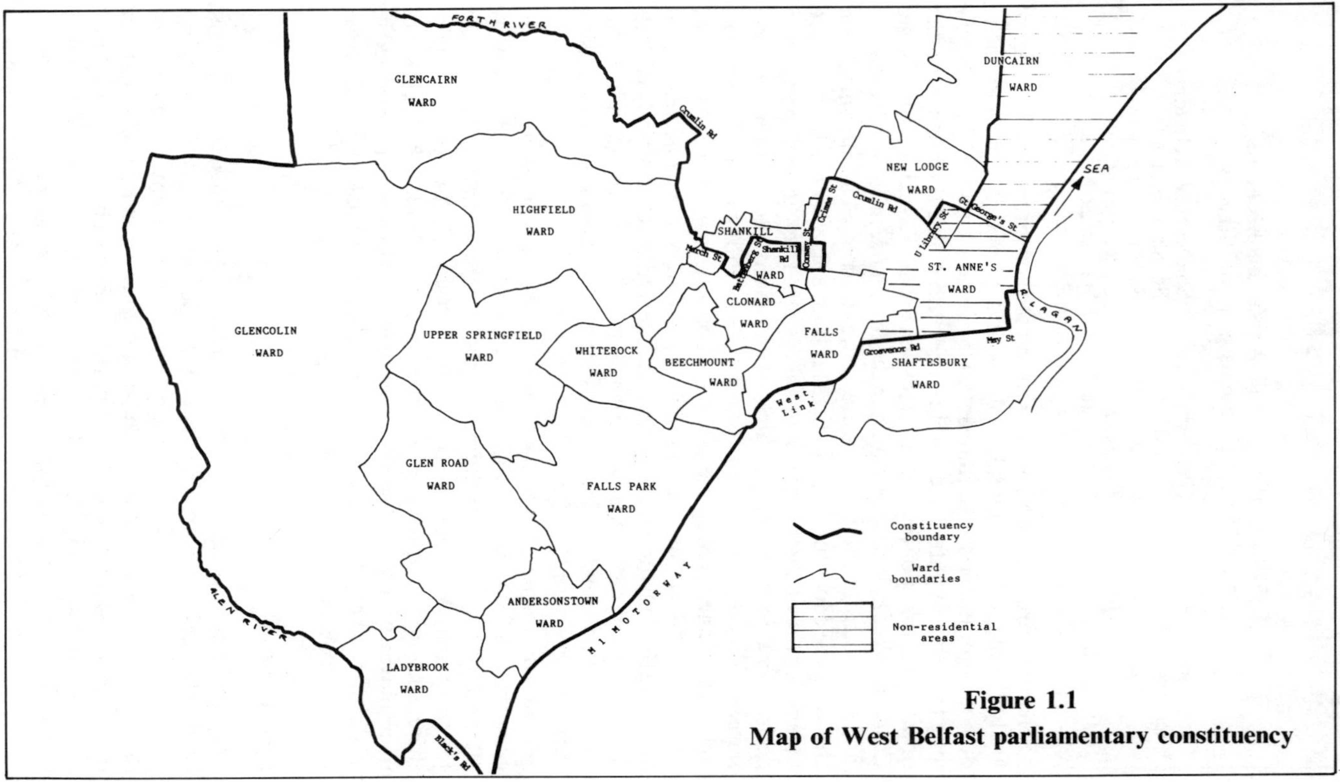

Figure 1.1
Map of West Belfast parliamentary constituency

Figure 1.2

Belfast District Council Wards comprising the West Belfast parliamentary constituency

Andersonstown	Glencairn	Shaftesbury (3 electors only)
Beechmount	Glen Road	Shankill (parts of)
Clonard	Glencolin	St. Anne's (parts of)
Falls	Highfield	Upper Springfield
Falls Park	Ladybrook	Whiterock

There are arguments against choosing the constituency as the unit of analysis. One is that economic realities, and specifically unemployment, do not begin and end at parliamentary boundaries, notwithstanding the long tradition of patronage within the British political system. Another objection is that political realities (*ie* divisions) are such that the larger Catholic West Belfast area would make for a more meaningful analysis. These are forceful points. There are, however, compelling arguments for choosing the constituency. Firstly, this is an area which is both defined by and a part of the formal political system. Even though power and decision-making has become highly centralized and to all intents and purposes divorced from the political system, voting is still, for the vast majority of unemployed people in the constituency, the only way they can or wish to express their political preferences. A second reason for choosing the constituency is pragmatic. The DED now routinely collects unemployment data on a constituency basis and there are indications that other government departments may move towards standardising their collection and analysis of statistics similarly.

As a constituency, West Belfast is a mainly Catholic area. But it also contains a substantial minority of Protestants who have been heavily affected by urban redevelopment, the recession and public sector retrenchment. Although the constituency is sharply divided politically, there can be no question of economic apartheid. The degree of unemployment in the Protestant areas demands that they be included in any economic reconstruction of West Belfast and hopefully these areas will join in the development debate.[7]

Report Outline

The report is divided into eleven chapters. After this introduction, Chapter 2 presents a brief history of West Belfast, focusing on patterns of employment and how the area relates to the economy of Belfast and the North of Ireland as a whole. Employment decline is a long-term phenomenon which has only been partly cushioned by transformations in the role of the public sector. Chapter 3 looks at how the commitment to full employment has come to be replaced by other priorities such as the defeat of inflation through monetary controls. The messages attached to monetarism are contrasted with some glaring examples of public sector subsidy of the North's industry.

In Chapter 4 some of the redistributive consequences of recent policies are placed alongside a discussion of the frequently stated myths about unemployed people and the causes of unemployment. This chapter also tackles the question of the relationship between political violence and unemployment. This is followed in Chapter 5 by a consideration of the arguments and policies surrounding sectarianism and unemployment.

Chapter 6 is concerned with estimating the true extent of unemployment in West Belfast, given that official statistics provide such a distorted picture. The constituency, and small areas within it, are contrasted with the unemployment position elsewhere in the city. The personal consequences of being unemployed are also touched on briefly in this chapter.

The following three chapters evaluate different aspects of the state's response to unemployment. Chapter 7 tackles the record of grant aid for industrial development in West Belfast. Notwithstanding the difficulties of obtaining data, the efforts of the Industrial Development Board (IDB) and the Local Enterprise Development Unit (LEDU) are scrutinised. In Chapter 8 it is the turn of international aid to come under the microscope. The agencies concerned are the European Community and the International Fund. We take a close look at what is spent and how spending decisions are influenced by government. Special employment measures and training are considered next in Chapter 9. In addition to assessing the scope and impact of these schemes in relation to West Belfast, the changing thinking behind them is examined.

As becomes clear from Chapters 7, 8 and 9, a number of community-based attempts to generate employment and services in West Belfast have been denied state financial assistance, or had it withdrawn. The origins of this policy are explored in Chapter 10. Some of these initiatives have had to contend with other forms of state obstruction. As is shown, the government's justification of this exclusion policy hides behind a single vague statement about 'furthering the aims of a paramilitary organisation' made by the Secretary of State in 1985.

In the final chapter we highlight the main arguments in the report before discussing the future of work in West Belfast. We discuss the costs of unemployment and the resources required to end unemployment. Some attention is given to the issues of defining and redistributing work, and the broad economic and political requirements for the reconstruction of West Belfast. Finally, we present a list of proposals which could provide an immediate response to the unemployment problem.

Footnotes

1. For the more articulate contributions to the debate about economic development in the context of Northern Ireland, see the following articles by Gaffikin, F. and Morrissey, M., 'Community Action and the Economy', *Scope*, April 1986, pp. 6-10; 'The Local Economy: Development in a Changing World', *Scope*, May 1986, pp. 12-15; 'The Economy: a Popular Alternative', *Scope*, June 1986, pp. 14-17; 'Economic Strategy in Northern Ireland: a Reply to Discussion (Part 1)', *Scope*, June 1987, pp. 6-8, and 'Part Two', *Scope*, July/August 1987, pp. 16-18; 'Bringing Cheer to a Depressed Economy', *Local Economy* 2(1), 1987; 'Popular Planning in Northern Ireland—A Viable Alternative?' *Local Economy* 2(2), 1987. See also: Blackman, T., 'Community Action and the Economy', *Scope*, October 1986, pp. 14-15; Christine, K., *et. al.*, 'Community Development and the Local Economy, Part 1', *Scope*, February 1987, pp. 6-8, and 'Part 2', *Scope*, March 1987, pp. 14-16; Neill, W. 'Optimism Versus Realism—Economic Development in Northern Ireland: A Reply to Mike Morrissey and Frank Gaffikin', *Local Economy* 2(4), 1988, pp. 314-322.
2. See *Fortnight* No. 265, pp. 12-13.
3. See references in *West Belfast: Some of the Facts behind the Issues*, Falls Community Council, 1987. Also, N. Gillespie, *The Vital Statistics: Shankill Employment Report*, Shankill Community Council, 1983 and Community Research Services, *A Social and Economic Profile of the Households in the Lower Shankill*, Belfast: Centre for the Unemployed, 1988.
4. *Belfast Areas of Special Social Need*, Report by Project Team, Belfast: H.M.S.O., 1976.
5. *Ibid.* p. 61.
6. See *Belfast Household Survey, 1978*, Belfast: Northern Ireland Housing Executive, 1979 and *Greater Belfast Area Household Survey, 1985*, Belfast: Northern Ireland Housing Executive, 1986. The *Northern Ireland Census, 1981* contains useful information but non-enumeration prevents detailed and accurate analysis.
7. The MP for West Belfast, Gerry Adams (Sinn Féin), expressed a similar view when he supported the *Obair* initiative in the following terms:

   'The Obair charter ... meets the needs of Nationalists in West Belfast who, for political reasons, have suffered over decades the denial of equality of opportunity in employment. It also serves the needs of non-Nationalists in West Belfast, for example on the Shankill Road where, because of Thatcherite economics, only 30% of the population is in employment.'

2.

West Belfast: The Rise and Decline of a Local Economy

Introduction

Whatever the problems of definition considered in Chapter 1, there is no denying that 'West Belfast' has an identity, not least in the minds of people who live there. Moreover, that identity goes back as far as the origins of mass industrialisation in the city. The area may have expanded massively since then, and indeed certain parts of it have contracted as we shall see; population shifts have occurred and the political boundaries have been redrawn frequently. However, for at least a century and a half there has been an identifiable area known as West Belfast which in many ways has been a microcosm of the industrial city of which it is a part.

The Emergence of Industrialisation

The origins of West Belfast's current condition ultimately lie in the differential effects throughout Ireland of the development of industrial capitalism in Britain. Britain was the 'first industrial nation', and the primary consequence of that for Ireland, its closest neighbour, was to create an economic division in the country between the industrial north east and the agriculture-based economy in the rest of the country. As British people moved from the land to become urban industrial workers, most of Ireland became the larder to feed that industrial work force. The Famine played a crucial part in the process, driving those it did not kill to industrialising countries like Britain where they became an essential element in the labour force.

The north east was the only part of Ireland where industry became established on a large scale. It was here that the plantation of Ireland had been most successful, and here that the strongest links—economic, political, social, familial and cultural—existed between Britain and colonial Ireland. The north east thus developed as an outpost of British industrialisation.

But industry in the north east was not as developed as it first appeared.

British politicians and industrialists had attempted through various means, legal and otherwise, to retard the development of potentially competitive industry in Ireland. As a result, the industry which emerged rested on an extremely narrow base. By the 19th century not only was the bulk of Irish trade to or through Britain, but Irish manufacturing in the north east had managed to develop only in those areas not already totally dominated by Britain, that is, linen and ship production. The north east's ruling class in the heyday of industrial production at the end of the 19th century could sing the praises of their economy, but the truth was it was far from healthy. It was overly dependent on Britain and in addition was not diversified enough to absorb the major changes in industrial production which were to occur in the 20th century.

Belfast became the hub of this economy. Yet, it was not a city in which everybody benefited equally from industrial growth. Like any emerging industrial city, it had its stark divisions along class lines, with those at the bottom of the hierarchy experiencing incredible levels of poverty and disease. But in addition it had an equally stark sectarian division.

As Belfast's population grew, so did its proportion of Catholics. By 1834 Catholics made up 32% of the 19,712 inhabitants. Twenty-five years later they reached their highest proportion—34% of the city's population of 41,406. Afterwards the proportion of Catholics declined, remaining somewhere between 23% and 26% from 1881 on into the middle of this century.[1] The high point in 1861 is no coincidence. Famine hit the agricultural and mainly Catholic parts of Ireland hardest. Belfast offered poverty, overcrowding and disease, but it also held out one prospect for starving Catholics that was like a flame for a moth—the prospect of work and therefore survival.

But what kind of work? Catholics had traditionally lived in the areas just west and north of the town centre before industrialisation. The sudden influx of Catholics coincided with Belfast's first stage of industrialisation, cotton and later linen production. Many of the linen mills were built adjacent to rivers which flowed through north and west Belfast, and so the Catholic residential area expanded alongside the factories. It was in what is now known as the Lower Falls that many of the Catholics who flocked to Belfast in the first half of the last century, and in particular Catholic women, found employment. And by the middle of the century the vast majority of Belfast's Catholics lived in the west of the city.

While the main wave of Catholic migration to Belfast was before 1860, Protestants made up the majority of those migrating after that date. The combined forces of famine, high rents and sectarian competition had driven the Catholics to the town. But for rural Protestants the experience of better land, friendly relations with landlords, particularly through their common membership of the Orange Order, and, most importantly, the fact that they often were able to make a supplementary income through the domestic weaving of linen, meant that they were only forced to migrate at a later stage. It was the growth of the mechanised linen industry in Belfast which was the trigger to their mass migration, spelling as it did the death of domestic weaving. Their arrival in Belfast coincided with the second wave of industrialisation—the emergence of shipbuilding and its ancillary industry, engineering. East Belfast expanded rapidly in the second half of the 19th century, and it was here that a large number of incoming Protestants found both employment and homes. But the Shankill area of West Belfast, an area of traditional Protestant residence previously, also expanded. One reason for this was the emergence of numerous street-end engineering factories[2] providing for Protestant men in West Belfast what the linen mills did for Catholic women, namely, employment in the immediate vicinity of home. But interestingly there also emerged the tradition of many skilled workers in the shipyards travelling to work from the Woodvale area to East Belfast.

Even before industrialisation, Belfast was segregated on sectarian grounds. And matching that geographical segregation there was also a sectarian division of labour. In 1820 the Lower Shankill was populated mainly by weavers, whereas West Belfast Catholics were already showing an increasing prominence as workers in the less skilled, less well paid hotel and drink trades.[3] As Catholics poured into Belfast between the 1820s and 1850s, the division between skilled Protestant manufacturing labour and unskilled Catholic service labour became more pronounced. Protestants maintained their hold on their relatively privileged positions and the threat that Catholics were seen to present became the basis for open sectarian hostility and rioting as the century progressed.[4] By 1881 Belfast's pattern of sectarian work practices was well established. Catholics made up 29% of the city's population, but only 17% of the legal profession, 10% of the medical profession, 7% of the engineering workers, 15% of the merchants and 8% of the brokers. Most starkly of all, while Catholics comprised 32% of those in the lower ranks of the army in the city, there were no Catholic army officers.[5] Such subordination was to prove remarkably unamenable to change.

Belfast in its Industrial Heyday

Between the 1880s and the First World War Belfast experienced the closest it has ever come to a 'golden age' of industrial development. At its height the linen industry was turning out a quarter of the world's entire production of linen. The shipyards—Workman Clark's ('the wee yard') and Harland and Wolff's—were an integral part of the British shipbuilding industry, together with yards in Birkenhead, Glasgow, Newcastle, Tilbury, *etc* turning out ships on which the trade of the empire survived. The bourgeoisie of Belfast saw their city as 'the Athens of the North', an unlikely metaphor which says more of their rosy vision than of the reality of a city divided along class, gender and sectarian lines. Beatrice Webb, the English social reformer, was able to see behind the hype to the divisions of the city. She complained in particular that Protestant male workers were 'contemptuous and indifferent to the Catholic labourers and women who were earning miserable wages in the shipyards and linen factories'.[6]

As Belfast reached its heyday the sectarian patterns in particular had been well and truly established. The 1901 Census revealed this in relation to the middle class. 'Protestants were increasingly diversified in public services, commerce and the professions, whereas the Catholic middle class remained heavily dependent on retail dealing alone'.[7] As for the working class, by 1901,

> 'fear of a Catholic engulfment, trade union hostility to cheap Catholic labour, unionist suspicion that Irish nationalism would undermine Belfast's prosperity and perhaps the vicious circle of initial poverty, narrowed effectively the roads to Catholic advancement. They were, for example, 32% of the general labourers, but only 7% of the skilled shipyard workers, 13% of the clerks and 12% of the managers and manufacturers.'[8]

What this meant for West Belfast can be shown by a brief consideration of the 1911 Census. This shows that 85% of Belfast's Catholics lived in the west of the city. Such a pronounced concentration had one major consequence. The Catholic population was over-dependent on one source of employment, linen production. 47% of Catholic women who worked did so in textile production. (The other main source of employment for Catholic women was domestic service.) Any decline in the linen industry would thus have large-scale effects on the employment patterns of the Catholic population. Some Catholic men worked in the linen mills. But by far the single biggest group of Catholic men in 1911—28%—were employed as general labourers. Of its very nature such work was casual and unstable. Equally so was work in the building trades, where 7% of West Belfast Catholic men worked. Slightly more stable was the transport trade—carters and haulers—which provided work for 11% of West Belfast Catholic men.[9]

Overall, more than half of the population in Catholic West Belfast in the first half of this century was employed either in textiles or as general unskilled labourers. Thus, even in the early part of the century, when employment was relatively easy to secure, workers in Catholic West Belfast were in a particularly vulnerable position.

In engineering, shipbuilding, carriage making and chemical production, the 'high tech' industries of the time, Catholics made up only 10% of the workforce. Conversely it was precisely in these sectors that Protestants, and particularly Protestant men, were over-represented. These were much more stable sectors than those in which Catholic males were concentrated, as well as being better paid and much more likely to be unionised.

It should not be presumed that every working class Protestant in West Belfast was in more skilled and better paid employment than every working class Catholic. On the other hand the general patterns are clear. Belfast, like any other industrial city at the time, had its gap between rich and poor, and for the working class that poverty meant a life of hard work, low pay and frequent unemployment. But within the working class there was a further division between Protestants and Catholics. At its most extreme this ensured the skilled Protestant shipyard or engineering worker at one end and the unskilled, casually employed Catholic general labourer at the other. In this sense West Belfast was a perfect reflection of the whole of Belfast.

Industrial Decline

As has been stated earlier, the base of industrialisation in the north east of Ireland was much narrower than was needed for a healthy, diversified and independent economy. Consequently, the history of the 20th century has been one of inevitable economic decline. The two World Wars offered brief respite from the overall tendency, but the fact is that the emergence of new products, new modes of transporting those products and the internationalisation of both capital and labour hit the northern economy a series of debilitating body blows. After the Second World War the North's traditional industries to all intents and purposes collapsed. Shipbuilding, engineering and textiles had employed approximately 40% of the total workforce in 1951; by 1971 they employed only 18%. Between 1950 and 1976 39,000 jobs in textile production were lost, that is, 54% of the total of all such jobs. But the number of textiles jobs held by women fell from 46,000 to 13,000, a drop of 72%. Worst of all, total employment in the linen industry itself, the heart of Catholic West Belfast industry, fell from 61,000 to 19,000. In short, 70% of the jobs on which Catholic West Belfast depended disappeared.

For Protestants the situation was little better. Workman Clark's closed in the 1930s never to reopen, its disappearance a harbinger of worse times to come. The number of jobs in shipbuilding and marine engineering fell from 24,000 in 1950 to 9,600 in 1976, a decline of 60%. One poignant symbol of this decline was the fate of a City Council sponsored mural painted in Woodvale in 1979. It depicted welders working in the shipyard. Local people vandalised the mural by carefully painting out the men using the same colour of paint as used in the background. Harland and Wolff's was still there, but many of the local men no longer were.

As Chapter 7 recounts in greater detail, the Unionist government belatedly responded to this disaster with a policy of grant aid to industry, and in particular to incoming industry. But, in line with what was fashionable in regional planning in Britain, that incoming industry in the 1960s and early 1970s was encouraged to locate in towns outside Belfast. Thus, although thousands of jobs were created, particularly in the synthetic fibres industry (an irony, given that the growth of that industry had been the major reason for the decline of the North's traditional textile industry), there were two problems with the regional policy. Firstly, it was a case of defensive action; the new jobs offset the job losses from traditional industry somewhat, but unemployment climbed inexorably. Secondly, the location of grant-aided industry outside of Belfast ensured that the city itself benefited little.

The specific effects on West Belfast were different for the Catholic and Protestant population. Overall the area received few of the grant-aided jobs; the only exception was in the mid-1970s with the building of the Kennedy Way Industrial Estate (see Chapter 7). In general, the new jobs which became available were skilled and semi-skilled jobs for men in predominantly Protestant towns such as Ballymena, Larne, Carrickfergus and Antrim. This meant that numerous young families from the Shankill moved to the growth centres. The end result was the rapid decline of the old tight-knit community which used to be the Shankill[10] and the emergence of a skewed population profile. The Shankill today contains an exceptionally large proportion of older people. In the Lower Shankill, for instance, 43% of households are 'elderly households' made up of one or two people of pensionable age. This compares with a figure of 28% for the Greater Belfast area as a whole.[11]

The Catholics of West Belfast did not have the same access to these new jobs. Given that, they were less likely than their Protestant counterparts to move to the growth centres. The consequence of this is that Catholic West Belfast's profile is much more diversified, and much more youthful, than that of the Shankill. The 1981 Census, unreliable as it is because of the extent of non-response, reveals that half the population of Catholic West Belfast is under the age of 25. Catholic West Belfast's current population profile also results from a massive population shift in the early 1970s, when as many as 60,000 people moved home due to intimidation in the aftermath of internment.[12] The majority of these people were Catholic, and they flocked to the security of Catholic West Belfast, which became as a result heavily overcrowded.

At its starkest the pattern during the 1960s was that as Catholic women of West Belfast lost their jobs in the mills the replacement jobs, all of them far away from West Belfast, were occupied by Protestant men. Catholic West Belfast's experience was thus different from that of Protestant West Belfast, but, despite that, the end result was severe economic decline in both parts of the area.

The area would have become an economic wasteland had it not been for one other factor in the post-war economy, the growth of the public sector. This meant that new jobs were available, many of them within the area itself, as the provision of education, health and welfare expanded.

Most obviously, the growth of the Royal Victoria Hospital in the heart of West Belfast meant the availability of thousands of jobs. At the lower levels of the job hierarchy many of these jobs were for women—as domestics, home helps, *etc.* The fact that there were at least some replacement jobs for women in their area was thus not unimportant. But they were quite different jobs from those their predecessors had in the linen mills, most obviously because many of them were part-time only.

Conclusion: the Terminal Decline of West Belfast?

Chapter 6 details the position in relation to unemployment in West Belfast today. It suffices to say here that levels of unemployment in the area have risen exorbitantly since the late 1970s due to two processes. Firstly, the jobs provided by incoming grant aided investment disappeared as the firms collapsed or relocated their operations in other parts of the world. Most obviously, the synthetic fibres giants left in quick succession, transferring production to more lucrative places like South East Asia. Secondly, the cuts in public sector employment which resulted from the monetarism of the Conservative government since 1979 eventually reached the North. In an economy which is so state dependent these cuts are potentially more drastic in employment terms than they are across the water.

What these processes meant for West Belfast can be easily summarised. The young Protestant men who moved with their families from the Shankill to Ballymena, *etc* in search of the new jobs did not move back when those jobs disappeared. Protestant West Belfast continued to be an area without industry and with a skewed population structure. For Catholic West Belfast cuts in public sector employment meant at their starkest that those women who had found work as home helps or as domestics in the Royal Victoria Hospital found themselves with fewer and fewer hours to work—and a consequent drop in earnings—or out of work altogether.

There is little on the horizon this time around in terms of job possibilities either inside or outside the area. Belfast's current consumer boom means some jobs, particularly for younger people, in retailing, distribution, *etc.* But the jobs are usually poorly paid, unstable and ultimately dependent on the boom lasting. Beyond that, the civil conflict since the early 1970s has seen a large growth in 'security-related' jobs, to the point that by 1984 one in every eleven Protestant males was employed in that sector. Once again, as many times in the past, the pattern emerges that while West Belfast overall experiences economic hardship, there are sectarian differences in the extent of that experience.

Footnotes

1. Budge, I. and O'Leary, C., *Belfast: Approach to Crisis*, London: Macmillan 1973: 32.

2. See Gillespie, N., *The Vital Statistics: Shankill Employment Report*, Belfast: Shankill Community Council, 1983.
3. Heatley, F., 'Community Relations and the Religious Geography, 1800-1860', in J. C. Beckett *et al*, *Belfast: The Making of the City*, Belfast: Appletree Press, 1983: 134.
4. *cf* Boyd, A., *Holy War in Belfast*, Tralee: Anvil Books, 1969.
5. Jones, E., *A Social Geography of Belfast*, London: Oxford University Press, 1960: 193.
6. Quoted in Bleakley, D., *Trade Union Beginnings in Belfast and District*, unpublished M.A. Thesis, Belfast: Queen's University, 1955, p. 33.
7. Hepburn, A. C., *Employment and Religion in Belfast 1901-1971*, Belfast: Fair Employment Agency, 1982.
8. Gribbon, S., *Edwardian Belfast: A Social Profile*, Belfast: Appletree Press, 1983: 47.
9. See McAteer, G., *Down the Falls*, Belfast: Falls Community Council, 1983.
10. See Wiener, R., *The Rape and Plunder of the Shankill*, Belfast: Farset Press, 1980.
11. Community Research Services, *A Social and Economic Profile of the Households in the Lower Shankill*, Belfast: Centre for the Unemployed, 1988.
12. Darby, J. and Morris, G., *Intimidation in Housing*, Belfast: Northern Ireland Community Relations Commission, February 1974.

3.

Full Employment, Unemployment and Economic Policy

This chapter examines the shift in economic policy which has accompanied the present recession. As an appendage of the British economy, the North of Ireland has been fully exposed to the new 'disciplines' of monetarism. But while some areas appear to have been abandoned by the state as a consequence, others continue to attract subsidies on a large scale.

Keynesian Economics and 'Full Employment'

From the 1940s until the late 1970s British economic policy was very largely based on a set of ideas made popular by John Maynard Keynes.[1] These ideas sought to challenge the classical economics of nineteenth century capitalism by rejecting the proposition that full employment should be or was the natural outcome of an unregulated free market. At the core of classical economics was a political theory about the role of the state in this unregulated market. Ideally, that role was to be minimal, one which would provide the basic framework of rules and law and order to enable manufacturers to operate as freely as possible. In reality, this conception of the minimal state was eroded continually throughout the last century as a result of political pressures from the more pragmatic and humanitarian elements of the middle and upper classes, and more importantly from the growth of working class organizations and socialist ideas. The experience of the 1920s and 1930s, and the political threat posed by mass unemployment in particular, led to a growing consensus amongst industrialists, politicians and civil servants that the state must play a much more interventionist role in organizing the society and economic activity. 'Keynesianism' provided the economic wing to the 'welfare state'.

Central to this welfare state was a political commitment to 'full employment'. In the (gender specific) language of William Beveridge, one of the principal architects of the British welfare state, full employment means,

> 'having always more vacant jobs than unemployed men, not slightly fewer jobs. It means that the jobs are at fair wages, of such a kind, and so located that the unemployed men can reasonably be

expected to take them; it means, by consequence, that the normal lag between losing one job and finding another will be very short.'[2]

This promise of plentiful work of a worthwhile kind, for which 'fair wages' would be paid, seemed to represent a substantial concession to the labour movement and, alongside universal social provisions, was popularly received. The state could guarantee full employment, Keynes argued, by ensuring that there was always sufficient demand to buy up all the goods and services being produced. It could do this by stimulating the private sector through grant-aid, tax cuts and low interest rates, and/or by increasing its own spending on benefits, services and public works, even if this meant running an unbalanced budget and hence having to borrow.[3]

In the North of Ireland, Keynesianism was late to take hold and never had a very firm grip. Agitations over unemployment and relief schemes in the years between the two world wars were largely met by force and a re-assertion of sectarianism, rather than by any growing spirit of consensus and compromise in the wake of such a severe unemployment crisis (see Table 3.1).[4] As it was, most Unionist politicians were ideologically opposed to the welfare state. The inter-war Unionist cabinet has been described as 'an executive committee of Northern industry and commerce with a few members of the landed gentry thrown in for good measure'[5] and the Unionist Party voted against the welfare state measures at Westminster. Because of the nature of the partition settlement, however, it was obliged to implement parallel legislation in the North. To do otherwise would have been to jeopardize the degree of political autonomy which Britain had granted and to call into question the volume of British subsidies on which the statelet had come to depend. Of course, many of the specific techniques associated with Keynesian economics were not available to the Stormont regime, having been given few taxation powers and being obliged in theory to maintain parity of provision and practice in relation to the major centralized social services such as health and social security.

Table 3.1: *UK Unemployment Rates 1923-1938, (percentages).*[6]

	1923	1926	1929	1932	1935	1938
England SE	9.2	5.4	5.6	14.3	8.1	8.0
England NW			13.3	25.8	19.7	
Northern Ireland	**18.2**	**23.2**	**14.8**	**27.2**	**24.8**	**28.3**
Scotland	14.3	16.4	12.1	27.7	21.3	16.3
Wales	6.4	18.0	19.3	36.5	31.2	24.7
GB	11.6	12.3	10.3	21.9	15.3	12.6
UK	11.7	12.5	10.4	22.1	15.5	12.9

As the post-war period progressed, the relatively high levels of unemployment which had characterised the Northern Ireland state since its creation remained a problem. During the Second World War the North recorded its lowest unemployment rate ever—3.4% in 1944. But after the war while the rest of Europe was enjoying economic expansion and heading for full employment, the North's economy was stagnant and unemployment rose. Not until the mid-1950s was the upward trend reversed and then rates fell slowly until the mid-1970s. Yet in spite of the flirtation with Keynesianism and the resulting attempts to restructure the economy and create jobs during this period, there remained a substantial difference in unemployment rates between the North and the more bouyant economies of the South of Ireland and Britain (see Tables 3.2 and 3.3). This differential remains during the 1980s, a decade which has witnessed economic recession on a global scale. In many respects, the current recession is more sustained and more severe than that of the 1930s.

Table 3.2: *UK Unemployment Rates 1939-1987, (percentages).*[7]

	1939 (July)	1947 (Dec)	1953 (Jan)	1968	1974	1979 (male)	1983	1987 (Dec)
England SE	4.9	1.0	1.4	1.6	1.5	4.6	9.5	6.5
England NW	10.9	2.0	1.9	2.4	3.5	8.4	15.7	12.0
Northern Ireland	**20.2**	**7.9**	**10.9**	**7.1**	**5.7**	**12.1**	**21.0**	**17.4**
Scotland	10.2	3.5	3.9	3.7	4.0	9.0	15.0	12.5
Wales	14.2	5.5	3.6	3.9	3.7	8.7	16.1	11.7
GB	197.5	2.0	2.2	2.4	2.6	6.6		9.2

Table 3.3: *Unemployment by Country—approximately comparable international rates.*[8]

	1974	1980	1984 (Nov)	1985 (Sept)	1986 (Sept)	1987 (Sept)
France	2.3	6.3	10.3	10.4	10.6	11.0
Germany (FRG)	2.7	3.1	7.3	7.9	7.4	7.3
Irish Republic	12.2	10.3	15.5	17.3	17.9	18.0
Northern Ireland	**5.7**	**13.7**	**20.3**	**21.4**	**18.6**	**18.2**
Sweden	2.0	2.0	2.9	2.6	2.8	1.6
UK	2.5	7.4	13.6	13.4	11.4	9.5
USA	5.6	7.0	7.2	7.1	7.0	5.9

Note: 1984 and 1985 UK figures are in fact for Great Britain. The 1974 Irish Republic figure (12.2%) shown is the 1975 rate.

Although official unemployment rates are now falling in some countries, few economic forecasters are optimistic about the employment outlook. There are already 16 million people unemployed in the 12 EEC countries and this is predicted to rise to 20 million in the 1990s.[9] But unemployment rates are not evenly distributed either between countries or within them. At present the officially recorded unemployment rate in the North of Ireland is over 2½ times the rate in the south east of England and 1½ times the Welsh rate. In March 1988 the North's unemployment was running at three times the rate in the USA and 11 times the Swedish rate. These variations have much to do with how governments have chosen to deal with unemployment[10] although the variations within state boundaries and between regions demand a more complex explanation.

Not only does unemployment diverge geographically, it is also unevenly distributed by social class, gender and age. Those under 25 years of age have suffered particularly during the present recession, not because of being made redundant, but because of the inability of the labour market to expand and accept new entrants.[11] But the most enduring and politically significant way that unemployment varies in the North of Ireland is in relation to nominal religion and because of the large degree of residential segregation, the sectarian division in unemployment rates is directly reflected in geographical variations, as illustrated in Tables 3.4 and 3.5. One of the most blighted areas in this respect is the Nationalist part of West Belfast.

Table 3.4: *Unemployment rates in selected travel to work areas, March 1988.*[12]

Ballymena	Belfast	Craigavon	Derry	Newry	Strabane	Northern Ireland
13.2	16.7	17.6	26.4	27.8	31.2	19.2

Table 3.5: *Variations in Unemployment Rates within Belfast.*[13]

		1978	1985
Belfast	East, inner	15.1	32.7
	East, outer	6.1	12.1
	West, inner	41.3	50.8
	West, outer	25.4	39.6
Belfast		14.2	24.1

Monetarism and Unemployment

Following Keynesian full employment principles, governments have, until recently, sought to influence the location of employment to mitigate the worst regional variations. They have done this through a mixture of tax and grant inducements to potential new investors, physical planning policies, infrastructure development and the provision of specialized services. As we shall see in Chapter 7, this has not always been to the benefit of the most depressed areas or to the most socially disadvantaged groups. During the late 1970s, however, the Keynesian consensus, such as it was, broke down and with it went many of the postwar assumptions regarding the state's role in job creation and location.

The new guiding principles, or rather what transpired to be rehashed old ones, are proudly proclaimed as a return to Victorian values. As has become all too familiar in parts of Europe and the USA, the repertoire of the new or radical Right, as it likes to be called, spreads across the economy, the political system, social welfare, and many other key areas affecting everyday life. The British government under Mrs. Thatcher's leadership is one of the foremost exponents of the post-welfare state society which some in government refer to as the 'opportunity state'.

Once again it is the role of the state which is at the heart of the revamped classical economics. The economic policy of the 1980s stresses non-interference by government, 'deregulation' and the opening up of free markets. On this basis there has been a rapid restructuring of the British economy on which the North is heavily dependent, much denationalisation and privatization of major industries, and major changes restricting the powers of trade unions. The Keynesian concern with full employment has been replaced by a preoccupation with 'sound money' and the 'evils of inflation'. Borrowing to support high demand has gone and in its place there is the goal of balancing the budget. At the same time, the state is interfering less with taxpayers by taxing them less, a claim analysed in Chapter 4. Given this agenda, social services have not only been cut back relative to the needs with which they must deal, but they have been subject to a 'cultural revolution' which seeks either to transform them into market-oriented businesses or to replace them with private agencies. Whatever the impact of international economic forces, these policies have been a recipe for unemployment. The monetarists claim, however, that in the longer term the market will deliver and full employment will return. For this 'natural rate' of unemployment, as they term it, to be low or nil, the free market must be permitted to operate without interference from trade unions or the state. But the labour market can only be fully deregulated, argue the monetarists, if there is a substantial reduction in social security benefits and greater discipline applied to the unemployed. Some of the right-wing radicals go so far as to claim that unemployment could be rapidly cured using such policies as restricting benefit levels to 70% of what an individual unemployed worker's take home pay could be.[14] Clearly this involves scrapping the idea of the state guaranteeing an adequate minimum standard of living for citizens (or a 'poverty line' below which no-one in theory should be allowed to fall). In practical political terms, it involves challenging the arguments and evidence of the poverty lobby that poverty is both widespread and on the increase.

This agenda has, however, been somewhat selectively pursued in the North of Ireland. Although the North's share of Regional Aid appears to have declined in the early 1980s (see Table 3.6), the industrial subsidy per employee in manufacturing industry remains three times the level in the north east of England. British Shipbuilders may have been almost completely privatized, but Belfast's Harland and Wolff continues to receive sizeable public subsidies, amounting to around £8,000 per shipyard worker per year in the mid-1980s and now approaching £15,000.[15] Together with Shorts (the aircraft and missile manufacturers), losses amounted to £115 million last year. Nearly a third of the industrial development budget for 1988/9 will go to the shipyard and Shorts which between them employ 11,500 workers.

The future of the shipyard is very much in doubt. All hopes were pinned on acquiring the contract from Ravi Tikoo to build his £260m boat 'the Ultimate Dream'. However, it was clear from the beginning that the government would have to subsidise the order to the tune of as much as £100m. Using the opportunity, they offered to sell off the company to Tikoo, having first written off its debts, estimated to be approximately £60m for each of the next three years. As union official Joe Bowers put it in a television interview, Tikoo was like someone going to buy a car and being inexplicably offered the whole showroom. He turned down the offer. The government is determined to privatise the shipyard, to the extent of holding back Ministry of Defence contracts and refusing any state subsidisation for any private orders until such time as privatisation occurs. This extra spur has led to management and workers to consider a joint buy out of the company. But the long-term survival of the Yard, despite government faith, would not seem to be guaranteed solely through privatisation.

The privatisation of plane makers Shorts is also on the cards, the government's determination enhanced by recent losses in the firm. Even the recent £34m order for ten Sherpa aircraft for the US National Guard will not of itself reverse the loss-making trend in the aircraft division of Shorts. Despite warnings from many sources, the government seems to be determined to sell off the company in sections. While this may guarantee the survival of the profitable weapons section of the company, it does not augur well for the plane-making operation.

Table 3.6: *Regional Aid, (including aid to nationalized industries).*[16]

Region	1979/80		1980/81		1981/82		1982/83	
	£m	%	£m	%	£m	%	£m	%
Northern	147.8	24	146.3	17	176.3	18	159.3	15
Scotland	117.9	19	182.8	22	220.1	23	370.9	35
Wales	104.3	17	170.8	20	198.2	21	181.7	17
Northern Ireland	103.5	17	138.2	16	110.8	12	146.1	14
Total UK	622.5	100	844.1	100	964.4	100	1,063.1	100

There are, therefore, signs of unease at the continuing dependence of major industries on government subsidies, a feeling which stretches to the general dependence of the North as a whole on British taxpayers. In 1987/8, state expenditure *not* financed out of taxation levied within the North, and hence having to be paid for by Britain, amounted to £1,569 million. This was equivalent to £28 for every adult and child in the UK. As one English MP complained recently, 'Northern Ireland gets five times the amount of help per person that we do, so why do the Northern Irish go on whining as they do?'[17]

On the other hand policies are being introduced which are very much in keeping with so-called 'supply-side' economics. One of the first measures of this kind was the establishment of enterprise zones, one of which straddles the 'peace line' in West Belfast.[18] The zones are supposed to allow industry to expand rapidly, unhindered by normal planning controls and exempt from local rates. A more recent and significant example concerns standard capital grants (SCG). Already restricted in size and scope in the mid-1980s, these grants ceased completely from March 1988 in line with the view that assistance should be more efficiently 'targeted'. SCGs were the only major remaining differential in industrial grant aid between the North and Great Britain. The CBI mourned the demise of the SCG in the following terms:

> 'We are saddened to note that an old friend which has served the Northern Ireland economy well for many years is to be wiped out ... The impact of standard capital grant has been very significant. Standard capital grant has supported development of many new manufacturers, helped existing companies expand and has been supportive of re-equipping much of Ulster's industry'.[19]

Another example is the introduction of the Wages (Northern Ireland) Order which amongst other things will restrict the powers and scope of wages councils effecting around 31,000 low paid workers, 62% of whom are women. Wages council protection is to be removed entirely from workers under the age of 21. This is yet one more example of the 'advantages' of parity—similar legislation was introduced in Britain in 1986. Well before this measure was adopted, the British government was being criticised for 'definitely failing to comply' with the Council of Europe's European Social Charter drawn up in 1961. This Charter was an attempt to guarantee nineteen 'fundamental social and economic rights', including the right to 'fair remuneration', which give workers and their families 'a decent standard of living'. The South of Ireland and the UK have both been censured as the poor nations of Europe, having been found to have the lowest wages in production and manufacturing measured in terms of overall labour costs. Britain's poorest workers are now worse off (relative to other workers) than they were one hundred years ago.[20] The 'free market', whether politically directed from Britain or the South, is moving Ireland closer to the status of a low wage economy more readily associated with developing 'third world' countries (see Figure 3.1). The recent proposal by the Belgian President of the European Community Council of Ministers for a European framework of minimum rights for workers, part-timers included, has been supported by all member states except the UK which is predictably hostile to the idea.[21]

Figure 3.1

Competing in the Third World

Linda Wachner, president and chief executive of Warnaco, the US company manufacturing underwear for Marks and Spencer at factories in Dromore and Keady, highly recommends the North of Ireland to any American company thinking of investing in Europe. Speaking of her company's operation in the North she said,

> 'We regard it as sound and well-integrated. The distance from our markets in Britain has not been a problem. There is a skilled labour force, and a great appetite for hard work. *It compares very favourably with our plants in the Far East or Central America.*'[22]

None of the assistance for industry, deregulation or the efforts of job promoting agencies have been able to reverse the decline in the number of people employed in manufacturing in the North which now stands well below the total officially recorded as unemployed. Employment of all kinds continues to be heavily dependent on the state. Over 40% of all employees are employed directly in public services while at least a further 20% are in jobs dependent on state support. The vast majority of household incomes in the North of Ireland derive directly or indirectly from the state, whether in the form of wages or benefits.

West Belfast is particularly reliant on the public sector for both jobs and benefits. The Royal Victoria Hospital currently employs around

1,750 ancillary workers most of whom live in West Belfast and three-quarters of whom are women. Notwithstanding its importance as an employer and provider of services, the hospital is being allowed to decline. About £1 million has been cut from the domestic services wage bill in the last few years. Two years ago management estimated that the hospital needed £12 million to be spent on repairs. Now the figure is approaching £18 million. In the current financial year, the Eastern Board has told the Royal group of hospitals it must cut a further £1.5 million.[23]

While the monetarists pursue their free-market fantasies at Westminster, the reality for the North of Ireland appears to be an increasingly state-dependent economy. But as the example of West Belfast shows, it is a dependence characterised by a public sector in enforced decline.

Footnotes

1. See Keynes, J. M., *General Theory of Employment, Interest and Money*, London: Macmillan, 1936.
2. Beveridge, W. H., *Full Employment in a Free Society*, London: Allen and Unwin, 1944, p. 18.
3. See Donaldson, P. *A Question of Economics*, Harmondsworth: Penguin Books, 1985.
4. See Munck, R. and Rolston, B., *Belfast in the Thirties: an oral history*, Belfast: Blackstaff Press, 1987. Also Devlin, P., *Yes We Have No Bananas: Outdoor Relief in Belfast 1920-39*, Belfast: Blackstaff Press, 1981.
5. O'Dowd, L., Rolston, B. and Tomlinson, M., *Northern Ireland: Between Civil Rights and Civil War*, London: CSE Books, 1980, p. 14.
6. Beveridge, *op. cit.* and Isles, K. and Cuthbert, N., *An Economic Survey of Northern Ireland*, Belfast: H.M.S.O., 1957.
7. Isles and Cuthbert, *op. cit.*; Moon, J. and Richardson, J., *Unemployment in the UK*, Aldershot: Gower, 1985; Trewsdale, J., *Unemployment in Northern Ireland, 1974-1979*, Belfast: Northern Ireland Economic Council, 1980; and *Unemployment Bulletin*.
8. Moon and Richardson, *op. cit.*; Trewsdale, *op. cit.*; Therborn, G., *Why Some Peoples are more Unemployed than Others: The Strange Paradox of Growth and Unemployment*, London: Verso, 1986; and *Unemployment Bulletin*.
9. *Guardian* 11/12/87 p. 25.
10. See Therborn *op. cit.*.
11. Ashton, D. N., *Unemployment under Capitalism: The Sociology of British and American Labour Markets*, Brighton: Wheatsheaf Books, 1986.
12. DED Press Notice. The rates shown in the table are for travel-to-work areas, only available on an old 'employee basis'. The new rate is based on the 'working population'. Thus the March 1988 unemployment rate for Northern Ireland is officially 17.3%, not 19.2% as shown here.
13. Northern Ireland Housing Exective, *Greater Belfast Area Household Survey 1985*, Belfast, 1986.
14. Hansard WA 6/2/87, col. 835.

15. Rowthorn, B., 'Northern Ireland: An Economy in Crisis', in Teague, P., (ed) *Beyond the Rhetoric: Politics, the Economy and Social Policy in Northern Ireland*, London: Lawrence and Wishart, 1987, pp.111-135.
16. Hansard Debates 8/3/88, col. 289.
17. Hansard Debates 8/3/88, col. 289.
18. See O'Dowd, L. and Rolston, B., 'Bringing Hong Kong to Belfast? The Case of an Enterprise Zone', *International Journal of Urban and Regional Research* 9(1), 1985, pp. 218-232.
19. Hansard Debates 8/3/88, col. 283.
20. McMahon, G. 'Ireland and Britain—Minimum Wages in the Poor Nations of Europe', *Low Pay Review* No. 30, 1987, pp. 13-20.
21. *Low Pay Review* No. 31, 1987, p. 39-40.
22. *Ulster Business* June, 1988, p. 19.
23. See Royal Group of Hospitals Unit of Management, *Ideas for Savings—Financial Year 1988/9.*

4.

Economic Practice and Social Prejudice

Not only has monetarism meant higher levels of unemployment, but it has also magnified differences in income levels, as is illustrated below. The main purpose of this chapter is, however, to show that the widening of inequalities has been accompanied by the promotion of a social doctrine which in essence puts the blame for unemployment on the unemployed themselves. In addition we examine the argument that the IRA are to a large extent responsible for the North's unemployment.

The 'Free Market' and Inequality

Whatever the mood of confidence and economic optimism emanating from the South East of England, to most of the North's unemployed it feels like lack of business as usual. There is now strong evidence that the 'free market' is acting to geographically polarize economic activity and resulting standards of living. Between 1976 and 1986 the discrepancy between the Gross Domestic Product per head in the South East of England and the North of Ireland rose from 39 per cent to 70 per cent. In 1986 personal disposable income per head in the South East was 113 per cent of the UK average; in the North, where average wages for men and women were the lowest, at £199.40 and £137.30 a week respectively, it was 76 per cent.[1] But such widening inequalities are taking place within areas as much as between them for two reasons. The first is that access to work appears to be more socially polarized. One commentator has referred to this as a new division between 'work-rich' households, where two or more adults are working full or part-time, and 'work-starved' households where there is neither work nor the prospect of it.[2] The second reason is that recent policies towards taxation and social security benefits have been entirely different. The former have been distinguished by their lavish generosity towards the rich while the latter are marked by a spirit of denial, meanness and discipline unrivalled since the infamous household means test of the 1930s.

The Chancellor believes he has achieved a veritable fiscal revolution which almost makes the UK the low tax capital of the world.[3] The myth is that everyone is better off because of the seemingly dramatic reductions in income tax. In fact marginal direct tax rates (national insurance contributions plus income tax) for the average UK employee are above those in France, Italy, the USA and Japan. Furthermore, those on 150 per cent of average earnings (£367 p.w., with a partner and two children) now pay more taxes than they did ten years ago because of the shift in the burden of taxation away from income and towards VAT and local rates. Those with incomes below this figure are progressively worse off the lower their earnings. The reductions in income tax rates which have occurred since 1979 have been used to further concentrate resources on the very rich. For instance the £2 billion given away by abolishing all higher rate income tax bands above 40 per cent in the March 1988 budget went to the richest 3.7 per cent of households in the UK. Meanwhile, the low paid, disproportionately concentrated in the North of Ireland and within areas such as West Belfast, are now paying nearly three times as much in direct taxes as they were in 1978/9.[4]

Coinciding with the budget has been the implementation of the 1986 Social Security Act. From April 1988, the total amount cut from the social security budget by the introduction of 'Income Suppport' is in excess of one billion pounds. For unemployed claimants, the arrival of income support is just the latest in a series of legal and administrative changes affecting their benefits. Unemployment benefit (payable on the basis of insurance contributions) is now so restrictive that only a minority of the North's unemployed receive it. The only alternative is the new income support (which replaces supplementary benefit). The loss of Single Payments and their replacement by the Social Fund under the new system will, irrespective of other restrictions, deprive claimants registered with the Andersonstown and Falls Road social security offices of £3.8 million in 1988/9. These are immediately identifiable cuts affecting each claimant to the tune of £220 per year. If the Shankill office is also included, the figure amounts to £4.6 million.[5]

Yet there was evidence of mounting debt problems well before the arrival of income support. Table 4.1, for instance, gives details of the amounts deducted at source from claimants' social security payments under the Payments for Debt (Emergency Provisions) Act (Northern Ireland) 1971 (direct deductions are also made from supplementary benefit/income support under 'normal' legislation). The total amount deducted from the benefits shown in the table in 1985/86 was more than £2 million, an increase of 81% on the 1978/79 total. The Payments for Debt Act was one of the last measures to be enacted before Stormont was replaced by direct rule from Westminster. It provides sweeping powers to make deductions from all forms of state payments (*eg* wages and benefits) and was introduced to defeat a strike of payments to the state, principally a rent strike, mounted as a protest at the introduction of internment without trial. There was already alarm at the numbers being compelled to survive on incomes below the basic rate of supplementary benefit during the late 1970s.[6] Now the concern is that advice agencies in areas such as West Belfast are swamped with debt-related problems.[7] Certainly, social security offices have been deluged

Cheap furniture (above) and cheap clothes (below) on the Falls Road.

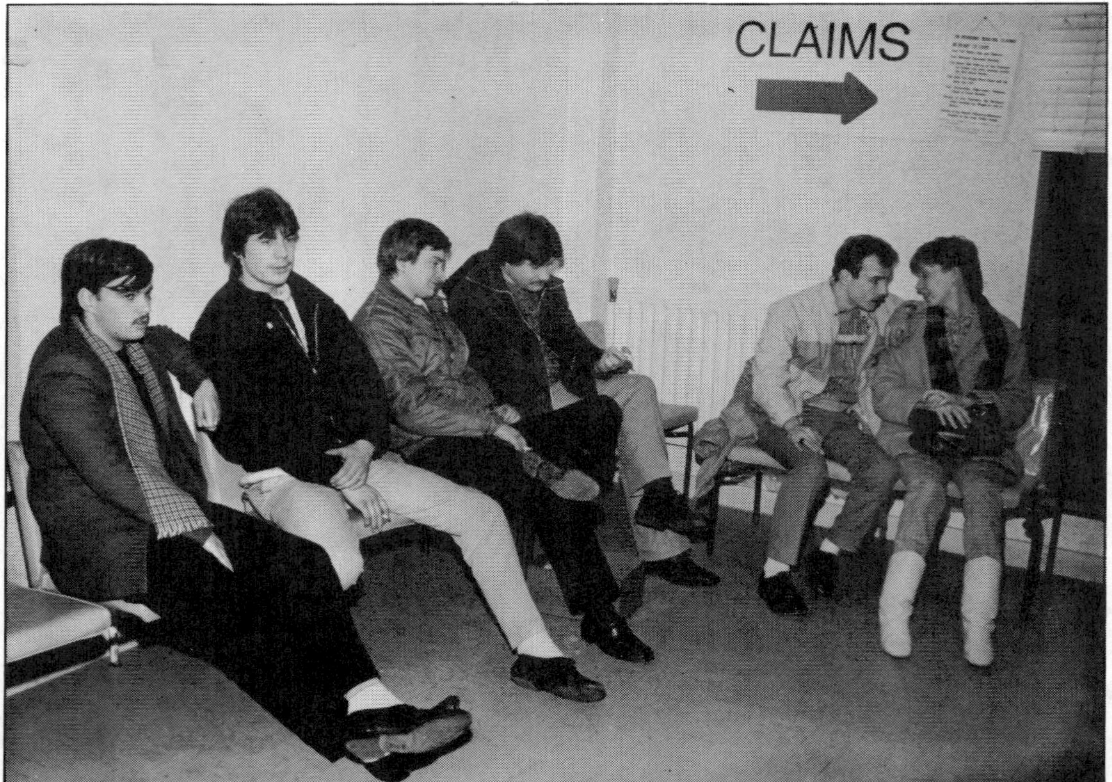

Waiting to sign on: Falls Road Social Security Office.

with inquiries from frustrated claimants prior to and since the introduction of income support, so much so that staff at the Andersonstown office went on strike to get additional staff.[8]

Table 4.1: *Direct Deductions from Social Security Benefits under the Payments for Debt (Emergency Provisions) Act, 1978/9 and 1985/6 (£000s).*[9]

	Supplementary Benefit	Child Benefit	Unemployment Benefit	Sickness Benefit	Invalidity Benefit	Retirement Benefit	Widow's Benefit
1978/9	764.3	11.8	122.4	12.7	132.3	39.8	60.3
1985/6	824.1	77.4	134.6	14.2	110.4	541.4	368.7
change %	+8	+556	+10	+12	−17	+1260	+511

Individualizing the Problem

In spite of this evidence of deteriorating living standards and concern over the future, particularly the unemployment and poverty consequences of the single European market in 1992, the rhetoric of the new economics and the social doctrines which go with it is regularly heard in the North, being taken up enthusiastically in some quarters. Regarding the unemployed, it is frequently asserted that they lack skills, or they live in the wrong place and are unwilling to travel to work, or they have the wrong attitudes, don't try hard enough and lack enterprise. The well-worn cliché is that they have demanded too much for their labour and priced themselves out of jobs. What was once regarded as a social problem, demanding institutional and policy changes, we are now being persuaded to see as a personal problem. The victims of unemployment are now held personally responsible for the decline of the North's economy. In short, unemployment is a cultural problem which will be cured by the 'enterprise culture' triumphing over the 'dependency culture'.

This individualist perspective informs the entire repertoire of government approaches to unemployment. Ill-health, for example, is no longer regarded in government circles as an inevitable product of unemployment, low living standards and poor social conditions, but is said to result from people choosing the wrong lifestyle—eating the wrong food, failing to exercise *etc.* As nutritionists have demonstrated, even if those existing on social security benefits were to follow all the official guidelines on what constitutes a healthy diet, their benefit would soon run out. The cost of a 'healthy diet' is, according to one estimate, 35% more than the average spent on food by low income families.[10] The implications of this are quite clear. Anyone on Income Support cannot afford a healthy diet and, at least to some extent, may be regarded as malnourished. In spite of the many sacrifices that adults, especially women, make we estimate that more than half of all children in West Belfast are being reared on inadequate diets as a direct consequence of low incomes. Moreover, this conclusion is confirmed by the findings of a recent survey of health in north and West Belfast which revealed that the area had the highest infant mortality rate in Northern Ireland, 11.9 per 1,000 live births.[11]

'Individualism' has also had an important influence on the extent and design of training schemes for young people and the long-term unemployed. The latest reform in this area, the introduction of a new adult training package from September 1988, explicitly sets out to 'equip the out-of-work with the skills to fill newly emerging jobs', secondly to 're-motivate those who have lost touch with the jobs market' and thirdly to put pressure on 'the significant numbers of claimants' who are 'not genuinely available for work'.[12] The specific impact of 'training' and special employment measures on West Belfast is discussed at length in Chapter 9.

These ideas have been so extensively aired that it is popularly believed that many unemployed people either do not wish to work because it would not pay them to do so, or that they really are working and claiming benefits at the same time—doing-the-double. Taking the first point, it has been recognised for many years that the financial incentive to work for persons who only have prospects of low paid work declines as family size increases. The problem arises because benefits for child support are lower for people in work than for people out of work. It is perhaps surprising that a government so concerned with incentives has failed to resolve this issue as part of its social security reforms in 1980 and 1988. The solution is simple enough and involves equalising the child benefit for those in and out of work, that is through changing the benefits system, not the attitudes of the unemployed. The vast majority of unemployed persons yearn for work and it is insulting to suggest otherwise.

The second point is not so straightforward. The extent of working while claiming is notoriously difficult to determine. From the limited available evidence, one thing is clear, however. The degree of benefit fraud of this kind is wildly exaggerated and, compared to tax and financial fraud, the sums involved are paltry. Regarding West Belfast, we can find no evidence that fraudulent claiming or prosecutions for fraud are untypically high or low. There is, however, one piece of research suggesting that supplementing one's benefit through casual earnings is more accepted as a way of life in West than in East Belfast. This is discussed in more detail below.

In recent months, the government has made much of the claim that investigation of social security fraud has led to the withdrawal of 80,000 benefit claims and 'savings' of £55 million. Particular occupations have been singled out for scrutiny such as building workers, dispatch riders, dockers, taxi drivers, market traders and hotel workers.[13] There is no doubt that the campaign against such workers has led to the withdrawal of a substantial number of claims. It is much less clear, however, whether all of these people were guilty of fraud and it is very likely that the £55 million figure is itself fraudulent.[14] If, as Norman Fowler has recently claimed, working while claiming is on the increase, this is probably the result of changes in the labour market, namely, the growth in part-time and casual work, and declining rates of pay and conditions of service. In other words, employers pay so badly in the expectation that people will subsidize their wages by continuing to claim benefit; and paying badly enough will ensure that employees will escape the attentions of the taxation and social security authorities. That is to say, the issue of working while claiming needs to be understood in terms of the nature of the economy in an area, including the opportunities for formal paid work. If the formal economy has all but collapsed then it might be reasonable to expect a less clear cut distinction, both in practice and in people's minds, between paid work and benefit. This is the argument put forward by Howe to explain the differences in attitudes he found between unemployed people in East and West Belfast.[15]

In any event in moral terms, the distinction between claiming while working for some extra casual earnings and working while signing on for a £5 or £10 addition to benefit, which is what is involved in the new adult training scheme to be launched in September 1988, is difficult to make. The conclusion must be that 'fraud drives' are a way of conditioning the electorate to support even harsher disciplinary measures against the unemployed. If the effect is to save a little money and to reduce the numbers recorded as unemployed then this will be fully in keeping with the government's general approach towards unemployment and the unemployed.

If we were to take seriously the objectives of stamping out fraud and making more efficient use of public resources, then we would do well to turn our attention to taxation. The evasion of income tax and VAT payments alone are reputed to cost the British exchequer £5,000 million per year. Yet Inland Revenue staff have been cut and the number of social security fraud officers increased. The treatment of the two types of fraud is quite different. Tax evasion is often admired by the rich and treated by many as a game. If it is discovered, there is no question of freezing the suspect's assets or business. The social security fraud suspect, however, will face the immediate withdrawal of benefit. It is hypocritical to attack claimants as 'scroungers' while condoning the illegal or dubious tax practices which form part of the costly and hidden welfare state of the rich.

Unemployment and Political Violence

So far we have sought to outline and contest key themes in the radical

Right's approach to unemployment by examining the impact of 'macro-economic' and social policies. There is, however, an additional dimension to the British government's understanding of unemployment in the North of Ireland which frequently crops up when the focus is on West Belfast. This is the claim that the IRA's campaign is responsible for unemployment in the area itself as well as in the North as a whole. The following statement by Nicholas Scott is fairly typical:

> 'The pattern of unemployment in West Belfast, in parts of Derry and Strabane and elsewhere reflects the IRA's hypocrisy when it complains about unemployment among Catholics in those towns and cities, yet *we know that it has contributed more than any other single factor to that unemployment in Northern Ireland.*'[16]

Similarly, in council chambers throughout the North, Sinn Féin is routinely accused of 'one day complaining about unemployment and the next blowing up a factory'.[17] As the debate about the economic development of West Belfast has hotted up, both Catholic church and SDLP leaders have joined Unionist politicians and British Ministers in attributing the North's unemployment to the IRA—'MPs unite in lashing IRA for job losses' run the headlines.[18] Bishop Cathal Daly, for example, has publicly argued that the IRA's strategy is to worsen the economic oppression of the communities which support it:

> 'The ideology of revolution, which the IRA share, is that the conditions of life of an oppressed people must worsen to the point where the sufferings become unbearable, for only then will the people see that nothing but total revolution will bring change and justice.'[19]

These statements are arguing that the IRA's campaign has a two-fold purpose in relation to the economy. The first is simply to raise the direct costs to Britain of its governance of the North through the destruction of people and property. The 'economic warfare' thesis is that these costs can be raised to such a point that British taxpayers will bring pressure to bear for withdrawal. The second argument is that unemployment is good for IRA recruitment.

In 1983 the New Ireland Forum adopted a report entitled 'The Cost of Violence arising from the Northern Ireland Crisis since 1969'.[20] This was a short report but it remains the most comprehensive available to date from which to assess the above issues. Before discussing the report, two points need to be emphasized. Firstly, the report makes no distinction between the costs of Loyalist paramilitary violence, INLA violence, IRA violence, British Army violence, UDR violence and RUC violence. Secondly, many of the report's figures are speculative estimates based on assumptions about what would have happened if the 1970s had been like the 1960s, or if the North's economic relationship to Britain was a fixed one. As the report itself states, 'any quantitative expression of the *amount* of loss attributable to violence is necessarily arbitrary'.[21]

The Forum report ranges over both general and specific areas. The inability to maintain the electricity North-South interconnector because of bomb damage, for instance, is estimated to have cost the North IR£180 million and the South IR£20 million in additional capital expenditure. Tourism in the whole of Ireland lost out to the tune of IR£2,280 million between 1969 and 1983, it is claimed. But the real argument concerns the general economic effects of the North's political instability, whether this is expressed in terms of lost jobs, jobs not gained, or a monetary value for lost output. In the 1960s the North's gross domestic product (GDP) grew on average by about 40% more than the British GDP growth rate. If this comparison had remained true for the 1970s then the North's GDP would have grown by 2% each year (between 1970 and 1982). As it turned out, growth averaged only 0.6%, so the Forum report concludes that there was an annual average loss of 1.4% of GDP growth. The report goes on to conclude that some £3,490 million has been lost in output between 1969 and 1982 because of violence. This represents a gross 'loss' of jobs in manufacturing of around 40,000 over the same period.

Another calculation in the Forum report, and one which directly concerns the 'economic warfare' argument, is the figure for 'criminal injuries compensation', a category which includes compensation for injuries (or deaths) as well as for damage to property. In 1982 prices, the cumulative total amounted to £1,008 million, although this excludes the cost of damage to government premises. But neither with this item nor with the general figure for lost output does the Forum report attempt a breakdown of costs which are specifically due to IRA actions. Nevertheless, as we have seen, some commentators have little hesitation in attributing all violence and its economic consequences to the IRA. In doing so, they are making a political judgement about the causes of the conflict in the North, not an economic judgement about the recession and unemployment.

It is also unclear as to what comprises the lost output or lost jobs figure—losses due to closures, a failure to expand output, or the inability to stimulate or attract new investment. The Forum report examined the economic impact of violence at the most general level possible, GDP growth rates. But at a more specific level of analysis, the relationship between violence and economic activity is much more difficult to chart. There are no readily available data on the number of businesses which have closed because of malicious damage to premises or as a result of threats, deaths and injuries to owners and workers, although one economist addressing a Confederation of British Industry conference in the early 1980s said he could not find any evidence 'that the troubles had been a major factor in the closure of existing businesses'.[22] Again, it is hard to see how specific acts of violence might have prevented expansion of output in particular businesses except at the most general level of business confidence and market conditions (see Figure 4.1). Having said this, there are some obvious exceptions such as the bombing of town centres, particularly Belfast in the 1970s, or when buses and trains have been targeted. A more contemporary exception is the IRA campaign against companies and contractors servicing the British Army, the UDR and the RUC, some of whom have made public declarations that they will no longer supply them. In terms of economic effects, however, it must be presumed that one contractor's loss is another's gain. The repair or building of RUC stations would appear to have been particularly effected by this campaign, with some suggestions that building contractors have had to be flown in from England to keep work going. Hence one consequence of the campaign may be a minor jobs displacement effect from the North to England. The only evidence we have come across that has any bearing at all on the effects of this campaign is in relation to the killing of building contractors and their staff. From 1985 until early 1988 there were six such killings attributed to the IRA and four to Loyalist groups.[23]

Figure 4.1

Investment in Derry

At the end of August 1988 the *Independent* newspaper claimed that two companies, one French, the other Korean, which had been considering investing £7m in Derry, thus creating 800 jobs, were having second thoughts because of a recent bombing campaign. The Industrial Development Board refused to confirm or deny the story. On the other hand, the *Belfast Telegraph's* industrial correspondent, Reg Rea, presumably quoting IDB sources off the record, added an intelligent qualification to the *Independent's* story.

> 'Sometimes violence is suspected to have played a part, but often, given the investment decisions of companies in even more troubled areas, no good reason can be found for the apparent change of mind' (*Belfast Telegraph* 1/9/88).

There has been much more discussion of the last possible factor behind lost output and lost jobs (or rather jobs which might have been) cited above, namely the failure to secure new investment, whether local or from outside of the North. Reasoned assessments of the condition of the North's economy vary in the emphasis placed on what is variously called the 'armed conflict', the 'violence' and the 'troubles' in deterring inward investment. Most commentators cite 'political instability' as well as 'violence' as relevant factors, but in view of the present spate of statements blaming unemployment on the IRA, surprisingly little emphasis has been placed on violence as such. For example, referring to the 'cumulative effects of over a decade of violence, destruction and political instability on the private sector', Professor Gibson writes,

> 'the combination of these influences together with continuing

technological and other changes affecting relative competitiveness, and total dependence on imported and expensive energy fuels, have had profoundly adverse effects on the economy.'[24]

In their recent review of employment prospects Canning, Moore and Rhodes begin by arguing that the economic problems of the North 'are similar to other peripheral regions of the United Kingdom'. It is, therefore, 'a mistake to blame these economic problems on the troubles ... Political violence has played a relatively small role in the increase in unemployment experienced by the province during the 1970s and early 1980s.'[25] They go on to attribute the 'precipitous fall in manufacturing employment' since the early 1970s to two things, 'the national [British] decline of manufacturing and the intensification of the troubles'. These authors point out that the job loss of 40,000 quoted in the discussion of the Forum report above is not a true loss resulting from redundancies, but an estimate that manufacturing employment would have been this much more if the conflict had not deterred investment. Taking jobs as a whole, the authors suggest that,

> 'the "direct" effect of the troubles, on manufacturing and security related employment, amounts to a net loss of about 16,000 jobs ... However if we attribute the expansion of the public sector spending in the province to the troubles we must add a positive effect of perhaps 35,000 jobs ... This gives a net positive effect for the troubles of about 19,000 jobs.'[26]

Rowthorn takes a less benign view of the relationship between the political conflict and employment. He argues that the 'branch plant economy' which had developed by the end of the 1960s was extremely vulnerable when the recession struck:

> 'Although they are loathe to admit it in public, the conflict is almost certainly a factor helping to explain why so many firms have closed their branch plants in the province over the past decade or so.'[27]

Rowthorn is critical of the view, popular in the early 1980s, that the failure to attract new investment is largely an image problem and that outsiders are mistaken in their fear of investing in the North. 'The truth', he writes, 'is somewhat different.'

> 'There is armed conflict in the province, sectarian strife is rife and the political situation is unstable, and until a lasting political settlement is achieved, it is unlikely that Northern Ireland will ever attract new private investment from outside on a significant scale'.[28]

Support for this assessment comes from an IDB survey of 'top businessmen in the US, Britain and in Germany'. The risks attached to investing in the North were regarded as so severe by 58% of these businessmen that they would not even consider it as a location for new investment. The 'achievement of stability' was rated as the most important factor by 86%.[29] As another report published in the early 1980s put it, 'the harsh fact is that foreign investors require evidence of political stability to warrant the risk of capital investment in Northern Ireland'.[30]

British Ministers have rarely missed an opportunity to counter such views. Interviewed by the *Investors Chronicle* in 1979, Industry Minister Giles Shaw stated,

> 'the effect of the troubles on the operating of the economy, while significant in some areas, is negligible overall. The security situation has changed over a period of time—less factory bombings and urban atrocities and more violence and attacks on the security forces within the border areas and in one or two others.'[31]

Similarly, ardent free-marketeer Rhodes Boyson during his brief stint as Industry Minister told the *Belfast Telegraph*,

> 'I tell them (English industrialists) they can come here quite peacefully because the troubles are only affecting a small minority politically and religiously activated in certain ways. I tell them that they're safer in the streets of Belfast than anywhere else in the United Kingdom'.[32]

Even more eloquently, and more recently, Peter Viggers sang the praises of Northern Ireland to an audience in Boston.

> 'The violence, which is the focus of media attention, impacts very little on the industrial community in the Province. The biggest problem American companies face is when they try to relocate key executives away from Northern Ireland: the quality of life in NI—its schools, leisure facilities and unspoiled countryside—is so high, people don't want to leave.'[33]

Overall, this is a confusing picture but some clarity emerges when such statements are put in context. In particular, it is evident that politicians have different messages for different audiences. In their statements about the economy, British Ministers focus only on political violence rather than on any other manifestations of political instability. Moreover they tell outsiders that such violence has minimal effects; they tell those campaigning for jobs in West Belfast that the IRA is to blame for unemployment. That rhetoric is also echoed by the Catholic hierarchy.

The Forum report and the economists quoted above present a more sobre and considered picture. The estimated effects of the conflict on lost investment and output are about three times the cost of compensation payments for personal injuries and property damage. The proportion of the latter arising from IRA actions is not known, but evidently *the direct costs of the 'economic warfare' strategy are heavily outweighed by the estimated indirect costs in lost output arising from investment being deterred by the overall lack of political stability. As the economists make clear, it is the political situation in general rather than the armed conflict specifically which carries weight with potential investors.* This was brought out very clearly when developers threatened to withdraw from the massive Castle Court commercial development scheme in the centre of Belfast because of continuing Loyalist protests against the Hillsborough Agreement. The UWC strike provides a further example. In this sense, the inability of elected politicians in the North to even agree how they can exercise power, let alone the economic and social policies which might be pursued, is as much responsible for lost investment as the armed conflict.

This conclusion is very much in line with the latest mid-year review of the North's economy issued by the financial services group, Coopers and Lybrand. In presenting the review, a senior partner of the company stated that there was little industrialists could do to improve the economy until politicians reached a settlement. They would have to learn to compromise:

> 'I do despair that after 20 years of the Troubles that our political leaders still find the word "compromise" a dirty word in the English language.'[34]

There is little evidence to support the further argument that unemployment is of direct benefit to IRA recruitment. Even though it is widely believed in youth and community work circles that there is a strong connection between idleness and law breaking, this should not be confused with a commitment to political violence. Youth workers may be correct in thinking that the axing of programmes set up to contain vandalism, theft, joyriding and other anti-social activities will damage local communities and young people themselves, but to suggest that youth will thereby 'fall under the influence of paramilitaries' is more sensationalist than real.[35] The broad conclusion of studies of the unemployed is that joblessness leads to apathy and resignation, not activism. As for the North in particular, Brigadier Glover put it like this in the late 1970s,

> 'Our evidence of the calibre of rank and file terrorists does not support the view that they are merely mindless hooligans drawn from the unemployed and unemployable. PIRA now trains and uses its members with some care.'[36]

In summary, political instability has had a considerable impact on the ability of the North's economy to face the British and international recession. It is by no means the decisive factor in explaining high levels of unemployment, although it has exaggerated and accelerated existing trends such as the structural weakness of manufacturing industry and the growth of employment in public and private services.[37] Rowthorn suggests that the North now resembles a vast workhouse in which most of the inmates are engaged in servicing or controlling each other.

> 'Like the typical workhouse, it imports a great deal from the outside world whilst providing few exports in return; moreover, as in the case of a workhouse or prison, the gap between imports and exports is financed out of taxes and levied on the external population. This analogy ... is ... intended to illustrate the nature of Northern Ireland's relationship with the outside world: the total dependence of the province on external support and its inability to survive in its present form without that support.'[38]

Most economists appear to agree that an end to hostilities and a lasting political settlement provide the only real basis for the long-term economic recovery of the North. But this would not be a solution as such as Simpson warns:

> 'The most dangerous deception would be to argue that with an end to the troubles, the economic problems would disappear. Certainly any progress requires stability, but stability is only a start'.[39]

Footnotes

1. *Regional Trends*, London: HMSO, 1987.
2. Pahl, R., *Divisions of Labour*, Oxford, Basil Blackwell, 1984.
3. Lawson, N., *Tax Reform: the Government's Record*, London: Conservative Political Centre, 1988.
4. *Guardian* 8/6/88, p. 11 and *Low Pay Review* No. 33.
5. Compiled from data given in Hansard, WA 3/12/87. cols. 693-694, and Hansard, WA 16/12/87, col. 583.
6. Action on Debt, *Sticking the Knife in: Debt and Debt Collection in Northern Ireland*, Belfast, 1980.
7. *Belfast Telegraph* 7/6/88 and *Irish News* 8/6/88.
8. *Belfast Telegraph* 23/5/88.
9. Hansard, WA 22/2/88, cols. 85-6.
10. Cole-Hamilton, I. and Lang, T., *Tightening Belts: A Report on the Impact of Poverty on Food*, London: London Food Commission, 1986. See also Whitehead, M., *The Health Divide: Inequalities in Health in the 1980s*, London, Health Education Council, 1987, and Stitt, S., 'A Meagre, Cheap and Usually Unhealthy Diet', *Scope* No. 103, May, 1987, pp. 10-12.
11. Department of Community Medicine, Eastern Health and Social Services Board, *A Picture of Health?*, Belfast, 1988.
12. *Unemployment Bulletin*, No. 26, 1988.
13. *Guardian* 1/6/88.
14. Seemingly, such 'annual benefit savings' figures are calculated by arbitrarily multiplying the amounts involved in withdrawn claims by 52 weeks.

15. Howe, L., 'Unemployment: historical aspects of data collection and the black economy in Belfast', Belfast: Queen's University (mimeo), 1985. See also Howe, L., 'Unemployment, Doing the Double and Labour Markets in Belfast', in Curtin, C. and Wilson, T., (eds) *Ireland from Below: Social Change and Local Communities*, Dublin: Gill and Macmillan, 1988. For a discussion of the available evidence on working while claiming see Jenkins, R. and Harding, P., *Informal Economic Activity in Northern Ireland: A Review of the Literature*, PPRU Occasional Paper No. 15, Belfast: Department of Finance and Personnel, 1988.
16. Hansard 14/5/87, col.409. Our emphasis.
17. *Belfast Telegraph* 14/11/87.
18. Hansard, 10/12/87 and *Belfast Telegraph* 11/12/87.
19. *Irish News* 25/4/88.
20. New Ireland Forum, *The Cost of Violence arising from the Northern Ireland Crisis since 1969*, Dublin: Stationery Office, 1983.
21. *Ibid.* p.19.
22. John Simpson, see *Belfast Telegraph* 22/4/82.
23. Hansard WA 16/2/88, cols. 595-6. Without producing detailed evidence, journalist Eamonn Mallie claims that the IRA campaign against local construction firms had no effect at all. 'The government persuaded many local contractors that they should continue to work on the projects: high unemployment, guaranteed work and regular income influenced many hard-pressed contractors—from both traditions—to take the risk.' Mallie, E., 'The Provos' Resurgence: there's more to come', *Fortnight* 265, September 1988, p. 7.
24. Gibson, N., 'Political and Economic Integration', in D. Rea (ed.) *Political Co-operation in Divided Societies*, Dublin: Gill and Macmillan, 1983, pp. 104-5.
25. Canning, D., Moore, B., and Rhodes, J., 'Economic Growth: Problems and Prospects', in Teague, P., (ed.) *Beyond the Rhetoric: Politics, the Economy and Social Policy in Northern Ireland*, London: Lawrence and Wishart, 1987, p.211.
26. *Ibid.* p.225.
27. Rowthorn, B., 'Northern Ireland: An Economy in Crisis', in Teague, P., (ed) *Beyond the Rhetoric: Politics, the Economy and Social Policy in Northern Ireland*, London: Lawrence and Wishart, 1987, p. 116.
28. *Ibid.* p. 117.
29. *Belfast Telegraph* 21/10/82
30. *Unemployment: Recommendations for Action Within a Strategy for Economic Development*, Belfast, 1982.
31. *Investor's Chronicle* 5/10/79.
32. *Belfast Telegraph* 8/2/85.
33. Northern Ireland Information Service, Press Release, 17/10/88.
34. Noel Stewart, quoted in *Irish News*, 17/8/88.
35. See for example, 'Paramilitary Alert as Jobs Threat Looms' in *Irish News* 1/6/88.
36. Glover, J. M. *Northern Ireland: Future Terrorist Trends*, 1978; reproduced in full in Faligot, R. *Britain's Military Strategy in Ireland: The Kitson Experiment*, London: Zed Press, 1983, pp. 221-242.

37. See O'Dowd, L. 'Trends and Potential of the Service Sector in Northern Ireland', in P. Teague (ed.), *Beyond the Rhetoric: Politics, the Economy and Social Policy in Northern Ireland*, London: Lawrence and Wishart, 1987, pp. 183-210.
38. Rowthorn, B., 'Northern Ireland: An Economy in Crisis', in Teague, P., (ed) *Beyond the Rhetoric: Politics, the Economy and Social Policy in Northern Ireland*, London: Lawrence and Wishart, 1987, p. 118.
39. *Irish News* 18/1/79.

5.

Sectarianism and Unemployment

The problem of unemployment is more than one of economic policy and individualistic social doctrine. It also involves processes of discrimination which result in very different levels of unemployment within a given class or population.

Differences in Catholic and Protestant unemployment rates have been a matter for debate now for many years. In 1971, Catholic males were 2.62 times as likely to be unemployed as Protestant males. This was the ratio in spite of emigration from the North throughout the post-war years which was predominantly Catholic emigration. Almost 40,000 people of working age left the North between 1971 and 1981 according to the census, and although it would be wrong to presume that all of these would have been unemployed had they stayed, it is reasonable to argue that this movement has measurably reduced unemployment levels, particularly among Catholics.

Although there is widespread concern in the South of Ireland over emigration, and attempts to measure the precise rate, this is not the case in the North. The effect on the North's economy of emigration is a neglected subject, so we can only form an impression of what is happening from anecdotes collected during the course of this research. The building boom in the south of England is clearly attracting some labourers and skilled workers, repeating a pattern familiar in Irish history. It is also evident that the North is training and then losing engineers, technicians, computer operators, doctors, nurses, teachers, social workers, accountants and those trained in business administration. Then there would appear to be a process whereby the most highly qualified school leavers go on to universities in Britain and the South of Ireland, never to return. In short, some of the most educated and highly trained workers leave the North through lack of opportunities and the promise of living in a more stable social context.

In spite of the large rise in unemployment since 1979, the latest research on the unemployment differential shows that Catholic males are still about two and a half times as likely as Protestant males to be unemployed.[1] The Policy Studies Institute (PSI) pointed out that over the period of rapid unemployment increase, the proportion of Protestant men who were unemployed rose by 8% while the proportion of Catholic unemployed men rose by 18%. The PSI concluded that, 'the difference between Protestant and Catholic men is not, therefore, only a historic one. In addition, some process has generated a much greater *increase* in the rate of unemployment among Catholics than among Protestants over a period of about eight years.'[2]

Mountains of Unreason

There are still people who seem to believe that the disparity in unemployment rates between Catholics and Protestants is some kind of statistical aberration. There is, as it were, a sectarian myth that Catholics have themselves to blame for high unemployment rates and that these rates are probably a lie anyway. This myth comes in different guises. There is the bigoted version exemplified in a recent outburst by an MP who, in rejecting the 'unproven assertion' that Catholic unemployment is two and a half times that of Protestants, said 'if any such gap did exist it may be part of the Republican philosophy to bleed the British system dry'. He went on,

> 'Many evidently believe in sponging off the state and do not want to work while others defraud the state by doing the double ... Perhaps Tom King would like to publish the Protestant-R.C. ratio of those involved in fraud.'[3]

Such sentiments were even more strongly expressed following the decision by the Housing Executive to demolish the Divis flats complex in West Belfast. One editorial ran,

> 'The decision to demolish the stinking cesspool that is Divis can only be seen as yet another step in Britain's appeasement policy towards the rebellious minority ... They campaigned for years to have this concrete monolith built at the foot of Falls Road. Thirty years later they have turned it into a dirt-strewn slum ... A community that thrives on welfare hand-outs has no desire to work ... And when Divis comes tumbling down, where is the NIHE intending to accommodate these mealy-mouthed scavangers (sic)? ... will further encroachment into Protestant areas be on the agenda? Whichever way it goes, the memory of stench-filled Divis should remain in Protestant minds as a poignant reminder that this is the way we would all be expected to stagnate in any future "All-Ireland Socialist State".'[4]

But there is also a more plausibly argued sectarian myth which seeks to explain away economic inequalities in terms of 'cultural' features of the Catholic population such as fertility rates. The 1982 *Year Book of World Affairs*, for example, carried a piece which claimed that 'size of family ... and other traceable habits of Ulster Roman Catholics, are mathematically sufficient to account for Roman Catholic disadvantage in employment without any need to suppose a significant factor of discrimination. Furthermore, actual direct evidence of discrimination has not been forthcoming'.[5] (See also Figure 5.1.)

Figure 5.1

Cooper Slams Lecturer's 'Nonsense'[6]

A Queen's University academic who dismissed discrimination against Catholics as a myth was yesterday accused of 'spouting a nonsense' by the Fair Employment Agency. FEA Chairman Bob Cooper said Dr. Paul Compton's views were 'more like something you would read in a pornographic broad sheet of the political underworld rather than an academic treatise.'

In a paper delivered to a conference on ethnic conflict in Sri Lanka, Dr. Compton ... said Catholics were more likely to be unemployed than Protestants because of their social class, geographical location and a high Catholic birth rate ...

The favoured mechanism to explain job discrimination against Catholics does not stand up, claimed Dr. Compton in his paper, "The Conflict in Northern Ireland". But Mr. Cooper hit back by saying: 'It's a nonsense to say Catholic unemployment has nothing to do with discrimination. *It has everything to do with discrimination*' ...

Mr. Cooper said he did not think Dr. Compton's paper would be detrimental to the FEA's work but he said it would reinforce the prejudices of those who preferred to believe there was no active discrimination against Catholics ... Mr. Cooper told a conference in Cork that job discrimination would only be wiped out by bringing new industry, investment and employment to Catholic areas.

Table 5.1: *Catholic/Non-Catholic Unemployment Rates Compared to Various Regions.*[7]

1.	**Northern Ireland Catholics**	**30.2**
2.	Merseyside	19.5
3.	**Northern Ireland Average**	**19.1**
4.	Central Clydeside	19.1
5.	Tyne and Wear	18.2
6.	West Midlands	16.7
7.	Wales	14.8
8.	Rest of Northern England	14.4
9.	Greater Manchester	13.9
10.	South Yorkshire	13.4
11.	**Northern Ireland Non-Catholics**	**12.4**
12.	West Yorkshire	12.4
13.	Rest of Scotland	11.6
14.	Rest of Yorks and Humberside	11.4
15.	GB Average	11.3

The main proponent of the view that high Catholic unemployment has more to do with population trends than discrimination was unable to convince the PSI or the Standing Advisory Commission on Human Rights.[8] After an exhaustive examination of all possible explanations of the unemployment differential, both bodies agreed that 'religion is a major determinant of the rate of unemployment'.[9] Table 5.1 shows Catholic and non-Catholic unemployment rates ranked with those in various parts of Scotland, Wales and England for 1981. As can be seen, the rate for non-Catholics, although serious, was not especially high by British standards.

As those in the equality of opportunity industry are quick to point out, the association between religion and unemployment rates is not of itself proof that discrimination is at work. Under present legislation, it is notoriously difficult to prove that discrimination has taken place. It is also quite possible for a major company to employ very few Catholics and yet for experts to find 'no statistical evidence of discrimination or failure to afford equality of opportunity'.[10] The lack of systematic research evidence on contemporary discrimination has encouraged the view that discrimination is largely a phenomenon of the past. Unfortunately, one opportunity to test this theory was recently lost when the Standing Advisory Commission on Human Rights dissuaded the PSI from carrying out 'discrimination tests', a research technique which the Institute has successfully used on several occasions to measure the discrimination of white employers against black people in Britain.[11] For reasons which are unclear, the Commission decided that 'this would not be a suitable form of research to conduct at this time in Northern Ireland'.[12]

Personnel Practices and the MacBride Principles

It seems to us that, whatever other factors may be involved, in order to understand the relationship between religion and employment/unemployment patterns fully at least three processes must be taken into account. Firstly, importance must be attached to the accessibility of places of employment. This is determined by the historical location of new jobs and the location of job closures. Detailed evidence of the failure of job promotion agencies to invest in the West Belfast area is presented later on in Chapter 7, which also provides details of closures affecting the area.

The second process concerns how employers recruit, select, appoint and promote their staff (see Figure 5.2). The exclusionary practices of the past are now famous world-wide and, partly as a result, this area has received most attention from policy-makers. The latest plans for reform set out in the White Paper *Fair Employment in Northern Ireland* and due to become law by mid-1989, begin with a disappointing statement of aims and principles. Essentially, the government is putting forward the principle of 'equality of opportunity for all sections of the community'. This, it believes, will be achieved through the modernisation and professionalisation of personnel practices to be policed by a reformed Fair Employment Agency which will be known as the Fair Employment Commission. The White Paper shows a touching faith in meritocracy. History is littered with examples of how 'equal opportunities' provide little more than the opportunity to be unequal.

Figure 5.2

Selective Recruitment: One Man's Experience[13]

At a Public Inquiry into Unemployment sponsored by Springhill Community House, which took place at the Conway Mill in March 1983, one man told of his problems in getting a job over a decade before.

> 'I think I should begin when I first set out to look for a job and discovered that the fact that you are from the Falls Road was enough to disqualify you completely. What I done was, after 3-4 years of unemployment and all the horrors that that involves—and I can recall being very frustrated at the fact that I had holes in my boots and no decent clothes to go to the Plaza and do a bit of chasing—so I decided to go on the dole and try to enrol on a course of some kind. The only thing available was welding and I had no interest in that, but I went and did this welding course and, strangely enough, excelled at welding and became very expert at it. At this time they started sending me out for jobs and the one that sticks in my mind was a job in the Shipyard. There was a guy there who I thought was a quite intelligent man, until he found out where I came from, and that was after doing a welding test which he said was excellent. When I told him where I came from, the Falls Road, he said, "Well, what the fuck are you wasting my time for?", and those were his exact words, which I have always remembered.'

After a few jobs as a barman and working in a bookmaker's shop, he tried another tactic:

> 'I had learnt by then to start telling lies. What I done was, I filled in a form for the place where I am now employed and I put my school down as Kelvin and I met the personnel manager who took me into a workshop and introduced me to the local mafia, the local Orange Lodge. I got the job without even an interview, and that's the job I am in now, and the management are horrified at this character they hired twelve years ago.'

Although he had succeeded, he realised that the situation for Catholic workers who had come after him was less secure.

> 'When there was a surplus of jobs in the '69-'70 era, Catholics were started in Mackies, in the Shipyard and the place where I am employed. What happens is at the first rundown of the industry all the Catholics get paid off and the firm can argue that it is not a policy of discrimination against Catholics; they were last in, so they are first out.'

This would be a less forceful criticism perhaps if the government had shown itself to be more concerned with results or 'equality of outcome'. The only solid reference to results in the White Paper comes at the end where the government rejects the Standing Advisory Commission's recommendation that 'it should aim to achieve a substantial reduction in the differential rate of unemployment between Catholics and Protestants'. Recognising that, even in the North's depressed economy, the usual turnover in employment is in excess of 100,000 vacancies each year, the Commission suggested that,

> 'an interim target to aim for would be the reduction in differential between the male Catholic unemployment rate and the male Protestant unemployment rate from two and a half times to one and a half times within five years.'[14]

This proposal was turned down because 'to set a target in terms of levels of unemployment would be to ignore the importance of the many variable and unpredictable factors which determine the overall unemployment level in the community.' The White Paper continues:

> 'In addition, it would leave out of the reckoning the fact that the unemployment differential ... will be at least as strongly influenced by social, geographical and economic factors as by fair employment policies.'[15]

What the government seems to be saying here is that on the one hand its own free market economic and social policies cannot be relied on to reduce unemployment significantly, and on the other, those same policies have manifestly unequal results, making the closing of the gap between Protestants and Catholics improbable.

Economic inequalities run much deeper than unemployment rates, as the PSI has pointed out. The employment and hence income position of Catholic households is on average substantially different from Protestant households. 73% of Protestant men of working age have jobs compared to 54% of Catholics. Protestant women are more likely to be working than Catholic women, both full-time and part-time. Protestants are both more likely to have a wage earner in the household and a second wage earner. Protestant semi-skilled and unskilled workers get more overtime than Catholics in the same grades. Finally, Protestants and especially male Protestants tend to have jobs at higher levels than Catholics. For all these reasons, the average Protestant household enjoys a higher standard of living than the average Catholic household.[16]

This summarizes what the government's 'fair employment' proposals are up against. In addition to the encouragement of meritocratic personnel practices, the key reforms are compulsory religious monitoring of workforces with ten or more employees, covering an estimated 85% of all employees, 'affirmative action' and the introduction of 'contract compliance'. Essentially, the new legislation will require employers to register with the Commission and to monitor their workforces in the appropriate manner. For this they will receive a certificate. The standard of their personnel practices will be assessed according to a Code of Practice. This has yet to be written but basically the Code will show how to be a model fair employer. Failure to discharge statutory obligations under the Act may result in the withdrawal of certification, although the White Paper is unclear as to the full extent of these obligations and the degree to which elements of the Code of Practice will have the force of law. Without a certificate, an employer will not be eligible for government grants (precisely which ones, yet to be defined) and will be excluded from government tenders.

The White Paper illustrates what 'affirmative action' means as follows:

> 'In addition to the cessation of casual, haphazard and informal recruitment procedures, affirmative action measures should open up job opportunities to the widest possible pool of applicants. This could be done in a variety of ways. Employers could introduce special "outreach" training designed to facilitate the access of an under-represented section of the community (whether Protestant or Catholic) to employment or promotion opportunities. Similarly, employers could end the display of flags and emblems likely to give offence; broaden their schools contacts to ensure that they are drawing applications from both communities; end any requirements for specific educational qualifications which are not absolutely necessary for the job to be done; and end preferential treatment for certain types of youth organisation or service experience unless that experience or service is a valid criterion for the job to be done.'

Critics of the White Paper have understandably concluded that it lacks teeth and is principally aimed at countering enthusiasts of the MacBride principles in the US.[17] Most of the practices which it discusses are already part of the existing Fair Employment Agency's policies. A change of name and a redistribution of functions, principally through the setting up of an independent Fair Employment Tribunal to deal with individual cases of discrimination, hardly merits the description of 'tough action' to break the vicious circle of discrimination.[18] The only significant new legal requirement is the annual monitoring of workforces. How such information is interpreted and acted upon remains to be seen. Significantly, the only reaction from Unionists has been in relation to this power.[19]

Figure 5.3 illustrates the response of one supporter of the MacBride principles to the latest government proposals. The government's ability to generate hostility to the principles and to conceal their actual contents was made very clear in a recent survey of employers in the North. This showed that the vast majority (82%) of employers had heard of the

MacBride principles but that only 2% were actually aware of any of the details. Yet a sizeable proportion of employers knew they were against the principles, with 32% declaring them to be either 'fairly or very detrimental' to the North's economy.[20]

Figure 5.3

Patrick Doherty's Response to the White Paper[21]

'The Labour Party spokesperson on Northern Ireland, Kevin MacNamara, observed some months ago that the British government had spent more money to defeat the MacBride Principles than on stopping the publication of *Spycatcher*. This has been more than amply demonstrated by the no-expense-spared lobbying campaign against MacBride in the United States. American legislators have found themselves the beneficiaries of the largesse of the British taxpayer as they are feted at exclusive restaurants and offered all-expenses trips to Ireland and the UK ...

US legislators are frankly puzzled by the MacBride controversy. Why doesn't the British government support these principles? To American eyes at least, they represent "motherhood and apple pie". They embody traditional American principles of equality and mirror US affirmative action programmes which have gained wide acceptance over the last twenty years ...

It is difficult for Americans to understand why the government, if it is sincere about reducing inequality, refuses to endorse anti-discrimination measures which have proved effective in the US. British ministers talk of the MacBride Principles deterring investment, but if their own proposals are "more radical", as they say, how will imposition of the principles on US companies deter investment while their "tough new sanctions" will not? ...

The biggest problem Americans have with the new proposals is that the government's commitment to change remains in doubt. There are undoubtedly people in government who are sincerely interested in taking advantage of the political opening afforded by the MacBride campaign greatly to expand the government's role in combating inequality in the workplace. There are indications, however, that others continue to see discrimination primarily as a public relations problem. New legislation, in their view, is necessary only to defeat the MacBride campaign in the US and to take fair employment off the Anglo-Irish political agenda. Having accomplished that goal, lax enforcement can guarantee the effective maintenance of the status quo.'

The MacBride Principles themselves are listed in Figure 5.4.

Figure 5.4

The MacBride Principles

1. Increasing the representation of individuals from under-represented religious groups in the workforce including managerial, supervisory, administrative, clerical and technical jobs.
2. Adequate security for the protection of minority employees both at the workplace and while travelling to and from work.
3. The banning of provocative religious or political emblems from the workplace.
4. All job openings should be publicly advertised and special recruitment efforts should be made to attract applicants from under-represented religious groups.
5. Layoff, recall and termination procedures should not, in practice, favour particular religious groupings.
6. The abolition of job reservations, apprenticeship restrictions and differential employment criteria, which discriminate on the basis of religion or ethnic origin.
7. The development of training programmes that will prepare substantial numbers of current minority employees for skilled jobs, including the expansion of the existing programmes and the creation of new programmes to train, upgrade and improve the skills of minority employees.
8. The establishment of procedures to assess, identify and actively recruit minority employees with potential for further advancement.
9. The appointment of a senior management staff member to oversee the company's affirmative action efforts and the setting up of timetables to carry out affirmative action principles.

Intimidation

The third process which is important for understanding the relationship between religion and labour market position concerns intimidation in the workplace. Not only do certain employers have a long-standing record of not employing Catholics, but particular workplaces have acquired the reputation of hostile places where Catholics can expect anything from occasional verbal abuse and threats through to physical attack and even death. In academic and policy-making circles, these factors have been ambiguously dubbed 'the chill factor'. Is it that Catholics have 'gone cold' on applying to certain companies or that they are 'frozen out' of some workplaces?

The PSI carried out a survey of such 'perceptions and views' in 1986. This survey revealed that in Belfast 23% of Catholics and 10% of Protestants reported that they had been victims of sectarian attack. Although such attacks were found to be uncommon over the North as a whole, amongst young men in Belfast they were very common. Threats or attack in the workplace were found to be much less common than the experience of violence in the residential neighbourhood. 4% of Protestants and 7% of Catholics who had worked in the last ten years had experienced a bad or threatening atmosphere in the workplace and 7% of Protestants and Catholics knew of someone else who had been threatened at their workplace. The survey found that fear of intimidation was much more widespread than the actual experience of hostility.[22]

It would be wrong to conclude from this that the fear of intimidation is therefore out of proportion to the real threat. While it is the case that workplaces are generally less segregated than residential areas, apprehension over the larger places of work which *are* heavily segregated may be well-founded. There are clear indications that elements within a workforce can sustain intimidatory behaviour irrespective of the apparent attitude of management and trade unions. Figure 5.5 illustrates a recent episode at Shorts. In this case, a company desperate to secure US defence contracts assured Michael Stone, US Under-Secretary for the Army, that Catholics would represent 33% of its recruits by 1990. Yet it is unable to prevent the sort of crude sectarianism shown in Figures 5.5 and 5.6[23]

In this chapter we have drawn attention to three process which we believe to be directly responsible for Catholic/Protestant unemployment differentials—the location of new jobs and job losses, employer personnel practices, and intimidation. The proposed legislation ignores the first of these, seems likely to have limited effects on the second and even less on the third, given the indicated lack of legal obligations and enforcement.

Figure 5.5

Intimidation at Shorts

On the 26th of April, 1988, a leaflet was distributed within Shorts naming ten Catholic employees as 'Republican activists'. Those named were warned to leave the company and not to return or else their lives would be in danger. The leaflet also threatened anyone working with those who were named. An exact copy of the leaflet's text is reproduced below (names omitted).

THE PAPISTS INSIDE SHORTS

The following is a list of names of Republican activists working inside SHORTS.

TAKE NOTE YOU ARE GETTING ONE WARNING ONLY

(name) seen at bastard Brady's funeral, this Sinn Feiner tried to get at Cpl's Howes and Wood.

(name) shown ringed. High ranker in Shorts Catholic Protection Association.

(name) in a 'P' check this bastard came up as I.N.L.A. active.

(name) and (name), these two like to petrol bomb Prods from their houses.

(name) active in the I.R.S.P., the political wing of I.N.L.A.

(name) well known Sinn Fein worker, personal friend of Danny Morrison.

(name) half of this bitter bastards family is inside for I.R.A. crimes.

(name) comrade of (name), this boyo drinks in the Hatfield House well known haunt of Republicans active campaigner for the I.R.S.P.

(name), this manager has a very strange bedfellow, none other than Tom Hartley!

The above are only a few of the fenian bastards we have to work with. I for one am no longer prepared to tolerate their presence here.

Laughing at the deaths of Geordie Seawright and John McMichael, laughing at the dead of Eniskillen, laughing at the butchery of Cpl's Wood and Howes, laughing when our flags were torn down but most of all laughing at the Stupid Orange bastards who let them work alongside them. From now on anyone found fraterniseing with taigs will be deemed as wanting them to stay and dictate to, and threaten the lives of Loyalists in Shorts.

The aforementioned are advised not to return to Shorts or they and all collaborators will be dealt with.

GET OUT AND STAY OUT REPUBLICANS YOU'RETIME IS UP

Figure 5.6
Intimidation:
The Harland and Wolff Experience

Q: Was there much sectarianism or discimination in the course of your work at Harland and Wolff?

A: 'I can honestly say that the blokes I worked with never said anything to me. When you worked there, you just went in and did your work. You never talked about anything, about politics or if anybody was shot. You just knew to say nothing. Then when it came to knocking off time, you went your way and they went theirs.

Most other people on the boat don't know your religion. They talk freely. They just take you to be a Protestant. They take it for granted that everybody is a Protestant. The only ones who would know you as a Catholic would be the ones you work with. On a big boat there might be only six or seven of us Catholics among 400 or 500 men.'

Q: What happened to your brother?

A: 'Bobby was working on a boat. It was Friday night. The boat had to go out on Saturday morning. They asked the squad of 30 or 40 to work all night to get the boat ready. Our Bobby went down early that night. At 6.30 he booked in, Bobby and a Protestant fellow. They went into the big hut, the Portacabin where all the overalls were kept. The two of them put on their overalls and made a can of tea. Then at a quarter to seven the other workers started to drift in. Two men came to the door, one called McC and a man called GJ. Bobby saw them coming but he wasn't thinking that much. Bobby could see out of the side of his eye McC putting his hand down inside his coat and he pulled a knife out. Bobby saw the knife; it just came towards him. He ducked and it went right over his head, through his hair. He got the man by the arm and the two of them started to wrestle down the Portacabin. The other wee man who first went into the hut with Bobby, he froze; he couldn't move his arms. Everybody else got out of the hut. That just left Bobby, the two and the wee man sitting in the corner. Bobby was badly cut. He was fighting, wrestling with your man and the knife was cutting his wrists. Your man stuck the knife through his lung. Bobby didn't know at the time. There was nothing in the hut to use. There were usually chip hammers and stuff that you use for the boat—something you could defend yourself with. But there was nothing there. So, Bobby eventually got the two of them out of the door and he put the big wooden table against the door. He was wondering why he couldn't breathe; he didn't know his lung was punctured.

It was a real dark night. This was just the week before Christmas. So Bobby waited for a couple of minutes; he didn't know if they were away or not. The next minute they pushed the door open and came into the hut again. The wee man was still sitting. They said to him to get out of the hut. They said: "You've seen nothing. You don't know us·' Bobby said to the two of them: "What did I ever do on you?" You see, because these two guys worked with Bobby. They just said: "You know what you done, you bastard. We're going to kill you." So the two of them came at him again. There was a gas bottle with a fire on it. First of all he poured the can of tea over McC's head; it was the only thing he could get. Then he got the fire off the end of the gas bottle. He held the fire at them to keep the two of them off. There was a hell of a heat out of it. Eventually he got to the door and ran out. But on his overalls was a hood; they grabbed him by the hood and tried to pull him back into the hut. He broke away from them. There was about 16 or 17 blokes standing about outside the hut while this was going on. They made no attempt to help him.

There was a time-keeper's hut where Bobby had clocked in for work. He kicked the door in and jumped in there. There was what you call a dock scraper. It's for scraping the side of a boat. Bobby grabbed the hold of that. McC came to the door with a knife. But by that time a whole lot of people had started to come on to the job. The cars started to arrive. So the guys then knew that that was it. They just shouted to Bobby: "Bobby, you don't know us", and walked away. But somebody on the boat saw what happened and they must've phoned the harbour police.'

McC got twelve years and GJ ten for the attack on Bobby. But McC was released after a year because of lung cancer and died two years after that. GJ is due for release soon.

Footnotes

1. The ratio was 2.44 as recorded by the 1981 Census and 2.36 when measured by the Continuous Household Survey between 1983 and 1985. Smith, D. *Equality and Inequality in Northern Ireland: Part One, Employment and Unemployment*, London, Policy Studies Institute, 1987, pp. 16-17.
2. *Ibid.* p. 17.
3. Rev. William McCrea, DUP, quoted in *Irish News* 28/5/88.
4. *Ulster* October 1986, p. 3.
5. Shearman, H., 'Conflict in Northern Ireland', in *The Year Book of World Affairs 1982*, p. 192.
6. Taken from *Irish News* 5/8/88, p. 1.
7. Bob Rowthorn, 'Unemployment: the Widening Sectarian Gap' in *Fortnight* 16/12/85, pp. 4-5.
8. See Compton, P. 'Demographic and geographical aspects of the unemployment differential between Protestants and Roman Catholics in Northern Ireland', in P. Compton (ed.), *The Contemporary Population of Northern Ireland and Population-Related Issues*, Belfast: Queen's University, 1981.
9. Smith, D. *Equality and Inequality in Northern Ireland: Part One, Employment and Unemployment*, London, Policy Studies Institute, 1987, p. 39 and Standing Advisory Commission on Human Rights, *Religious and Political Discrimination and Equality of Opportunity in Northern Ireland: Report on Fair Employment*, London: HMSO, Cm. 237, 1987, pp. 24-35.
10. Statement by Industry Minister, Viggers, on the Tavistock Institute of Human Relations report on Short Brothers recruitment, selection and appointments practices; see Hansard WA 12/1/87 col. 58.
11. The tests simply involve a controlled experiment in which applicants (*eg* Afro-Carribean, Asian and White) apply for the same jobs to see who is most/least successful at getting replies to letters, calls for interviews, *etc.* See Brown, C. and Gay, P., *Racial Discrimination: 17 Years after the Act*, London: Policy Studies Institute, 1985.
12. Standing Advisory Commission on Human Rights, *Religious and Political Discrimination and Equality of Opportunity in Northern Ireland: Report on Fair Employment*, London: HMSO, Cm. 237, 1987, p. 34 and Smith, D. *Equality and Inequality in Northern Ireland: Part One, Employment and Unemployment*, London, Policy Studies Institute, 1987, p. 2.
13. Source: *Public Inquiry into Unemployment: Report, Belfast: Springhill Community House, 1983, pp. 71-2.*
14. *Standing Advisory Commission on Human Rights, Religious and Political Discrimination and Equality of Opportunity in Northern Ireland: Report on Fair Employment*, London: HMSO, Cm. 237, 1987, p. 42.
15. *Fair Employment in Northern Ireland*, London: HMSO, Cm. 380, 1988, p. 47.
16. See Smith, D. *Equality and Inequality in Northern Ireland: Part One, Employment and Unemployment*, London, Policy Studies Institute, 1987, pp. 59-70.
17. See for example 'Bias Knife Blunted on "public" Jobs', *Irish News* 28/5/88; 'SF in Attack on Jobs Bias Scheme', *Irish News* 8/6/88; and 'Fair Employment Backlash feared from Protestants', *Guardian* 25/5/88.

18. See ‘King Outlines “tough” Jobs Legislation’, *Irish News* 2/7/88.
19. See ‘Unionist Resentment at “religion” Clause’ and *Editorial* in *News Letter* 26/5/88.
20. ‘Employer attitudes towards religious discrimination in employment’, *Ulster Business* January 1988, pp. 20-23.
21. Patrick Doherty, ‘MacBride effort: US map keeps on getting darker’, *Fortnight* No. 264, July/August 1988, pp. 11-12.
22. Smith, D. *Equality and Inequality in Northern Ireland: Part Three, Perceptions and Views*, London, Policy Studies Institute, 1987.
23. *Belfast Telegraph* 1/7/88. See also the claim that Shorts has become ‘one of the biggest employers of Catholics in the province’, *Belfast Telegraph* 19/8/88.

6.

Figures, Facts and Fiction

This chapter reviews the available measures of unemployment and explains why the official statistics understate the problem. We also refer to the personal consequences of unemployment.

The cumulative effect of the three processes outlined in the previous chapter is to heavily disadvantage the majority of workers in West Belfast. As can be seen from Table 6.1, nearly a fifth of all the North's unemployment is to be found in the two parliamentary constituencies of Foyle (Derry) and West Belfast. Just under a tenth (9.4%) of the total unemployed live in West Belfast. When it comes to long-term unemployment, a slightly worse picture emerges, with 10.7% of those in the North without work for a year or more living in West Belfast.

Table 6.1: *Percentage Share of Unemployment in Selected Parliamentary Constituencies, March 1988.*[1]

Belfast East	3.9
Belfast North	6.8
Belfast South	4.8
Belfast West	**9.4**
East Antrim	5.1
Foyle	9.5
North Down	3.6
Strangford	3.4

One quarter of the North's unemployment is concentrated in the Belfast constituencies. But West Belfast carries 38% of Belfast's unemployment. Table 6.2 shows the burden of unemployment falling on different wards. From this it can be seen that the worst Protestant ward (Ballymacarrett) is only marginally worse than the best Catholic Ward (Andersonstown). The Upper Springfield ward has eight times as much of Belfast's unemployment as the Stormont ward.

Table 6.2: *Percentage Share of Unemployment within Belfast, Selected District Council Wards, February 1988.*[2]

EAST BELFAST	
Ballymacarrett	2.3
Stormont	0.5
Knock	0.9
Ravenhill	1.0
WEST BELFAST	
Falls	3.4
Upper Springfield	4.1
Andersonstown	2.1
Ladybrook	2.3
Whiterock	3.7

Even within West Belfast there are substantial variations. In many areas, over half the heads of households are unemployed and in places the rate climbs to more than 85%. Table 6.3 draws together various measures of unemployment gleaned from local surveys and benefit take-up campaigns. These figures are not strictly comparable but they do give a strong sense of the depth of work deprivation in some areas.

Table 6.3: *Rates of Unemployment Within West Belfast.*[3]

1983	Ballymurphy	86% (of all adults)
1986/7	Divis Flats (all)	67% (Male) 48% (Female)
1986/7	Lower Falls	61% (of all economically active)
1987	Lower Shankill	20% (of all adults)
1985	Moyard	79% (of all adults)
1986/7	Twinbrook (all)	46% (Male) 18% (Female)
1986/7	Unity Flats (of all economically active)	77% (Male) 40% (Female)

The severity of the situation is perhaps better illustrated by considering *employment* rather than unemployment rates. The *employment* rate is a measure of total employment expressed as a percentage of the population of working age. In 1983, the employment rates in Germany, the USA and UK were 59%, 66% and 64% respectively. In that same year, the employment rate was only 14% in Ballymurphy. In 1986 the employment rate for the Lower Falls was found to be 29%.

The Politics of Numbers

Most of the available statistics on unemployment are generated by the Department of Economic Development or rely on definitions of unemployment enshrined in the official figures. Long ago, the radical Right began to argue that the official count of the unemployed exaggerated the extent of the problem. This was significant because successive post-war governments had used the unemployment rate as a key economic indicator, for example responding to a rise in the rate with a 'Keynesian expansion' of demand. The Right argued that governments were being misled into inappropriate economic policies by unemployment figures which included many, such as students, the long-term sick, disabled and women, who were not really available or willing to work.

Figure 6.1

Wishing Away the Unemployed[4]

'It would be heartless to continue to pay benefit to those who do not take advantage of the wonderful opportunities that are being provided ... the greatest training aid that some people need is a well-placed boot up the backside.' Tony Marlow, MP, 18/11/87.

'And it is no use saying that the figures are really three million. I suspect there's a vast amount in there who could work if they wanted to. Now I'm not claiming, and make sure you don't cut this, there is not a group genuinely in need. What I am saying is there is a larger group than people will admit who are finding it very convenient to collect every single benefit God can give them earning a little bit over the end.' Jeffrey Archer, BBC Radio 4 interview, 5 October, 1985.

'Yes there are people outside the count both looking for work and taking jobs in large numbers, but there are also within the count—*almost a million*—who are either in paid employment or not seeking work at all.' Lord Young, *The Times*, 5/10/85.

'I'm not losing sleep about the future of unemployment. I am losing sleep about incentives to get people back to work ... forget the type of job.' Lord Young, Channel 4 News, 12/2/87.

'For the 87% in work, the country has never had as good a time as it has today.' Lord Young.

'Perhaps we should be a little tougher on the benefits in those areas where there are jobs ... some people find life on the safety net a little too comfortable.' Norman Tebbit.

The statistics were also flawed as an indicator of the true state of the labour market, the Right claimed, because they included so many people between jobs and so many 'scroungers' who never intend to work. Using such arguments and reclassifications commentators could magically reduce both the total numbers officially counted as unemployed and the unemployment rate itself. The sentiments involved are clearly illustrated in Figure 6.1.

Since 1979 there have been twenty four changes which have directly effected the unemployment count. Some of these have been to do with the actual method of counting while others have been concerned with benefit eligibility and the way in which work availability is tested. Figure 6.2 lists some of the changes that have been implemented in the North between 1981 and 1986.

Figure 6.2

Changes in the Presentation of Unemployment Statistics, 1981 to 1986.[5]

1. 1981: Changed benefit regulations mean that June school leavers cannot claim benefit until September when they are included in the count. For June, July and August each year a special count of school leavers registered at jobmarkets is provided.
2. 1981: Introduction of long-term rate of supplementary benefit for males aged 60+ on supplementary benefit for over one year—such people formerly 'unemployed', now 'retired'.
3. 1982: Changes of basis for unemployment statistics from registrants at Employment Service Offices to claimants of benefit at DHSS Social Security Offices. Count reduced substantially.
4. 1983: Budget measures gave males aged 60 and over: a) the long-term rate of supplementary benefit without waiting one year, b) automatic National Insurance credits without signing on—such persons therefore excluded from the unemployment count.
5. 1984: Unemployment figures for the revised travel-to-work areas produced.
6. 1985: Reconciliation of DED computer records with DHSS manual records—reduced count.
7. 1986: Unemployment figures compiled each month two weeks later than previously—reduces count.
8. 1986: Additional unemployment rate introduced based on employees in employment, unemployed, self-employed and armed forces ('the working population'). Reduces rate considerably.
9. 1986: Right to half and three-quarter rate unemployment benefit for those unable to qualify for full unemployment benefit abolished. Excludes many women from the count.

One of the most significant changes was the move to a count of claimants rather than job centre registrants in 1982. In other words since 1982 people are only counted as unemployed if they receive benefit as an unemployed person. You are not officially unemployed if your partner receives benefit on your behalf or you are not directly in receipt of benefit for some other reason. In practice, this has served to exclude many women and young people from the ranks of the officially unemployed. All of the changes which followed this move to a claimant-based count have resulted in a downwards revision of the unemployment figures. In the latest change to be announced, summer school leavers are no longer counted and soon no-one under 18 will be counted. In Britain this will have the effect of excluding 100,000 young people from the total unemployed.[6] This statistical liquidation of youth unemployment can be readily seen from the data in Table 6.4.

Table 6.4: *Unemployed Aged under 18 in the North of Ireland, 1982-87.* [7]

1982 July	(registrants)	12,203
1982 Oct	(registrants)	11,037
1982 Oct	(claimants)	9,000
1983 Oct	(claimants)	7,841
1984 Oct	(claimants)	6,614
1985 Oct	(claimants)	5,895
1986 Oct	(claimants)	5,940
1987 Jan	(latest available figure)	4,696

Another change which appears to be having a significant affect on the official figures is the new availability for work test. Unemployed claimants must answer 17 questions designed to check if they are really looking for work. The rules underpinning the questionnaire amongst other things require claimants to be prepared to work on Saturdays and to travel greater, though unspecified, distances than previously. Claimants must be able to start work immediately, show evidence that they are actively seeking work and should consider taking work which is not their normal occupation and at a lower wage than their last job.[8] Such testing is resulting in some unemployed people being reclassified as 'sick' and some having their availability questioned. The latter may lead to suspension of benefit and thus the removal of the person from the count, if only temporarily. The questioning of an unemployed person's availability for work used to lead to an immediate suspension of benefit, although this is no longer supposed to happen due to a change in policy prompted by the widespread publicity given to the letter shown in Figure 6.3.

Figure 6.3

Letter written by Rachel Caine who killed herself after her benefit was withdrawn[9]

'Dear Home Secretary,

I am writing to inform you that another embarrassing statistic has chosen the "opting out" clause offered by the constitution—by deciding on suicide rather than going on with the rigmarole of trying to grub a living under the system.

I don't harbour any ill-will towards the system and fully agree that the burden of keeping me alive is frankly neither cost-effective nor worthwhile.

Although for the past 20 years I have struggled to earn a crust (under the delusion that survival was worthwhile at any cost) in all sorts of jobs—some of them very menial and badly paid—now that the Department of Health and Social Security has deemed me unfit to be supported, I must say I see the wisdom of their decision ...'

The London-based Unemployment Unit has for some years produced an alternative index of unemployment. This gives a measure of what the count would be had the government continued to base figures on job centre registrants. For March 1988, for example, the DED figures suggested that 116,500 were unemployed (seasonally adjusted) in the North of Ireland, giving an unemployment rate of 17.1%. The Unemployment Unit's index (seasonally adjusted) indicates that there are 147,000 unemployed and the rate is 23.2%. Such estimates suggest that instead of there being 11,857 unemployed persons in West Belfast in November 1987, as reported officially, the figure was closer to 15,000. In any event, both old and new methods seriously understate the numbers of women seeking work so the true measure of unemployment for the constituency at that time was likely to exceed this comfortably.

The Unemployment Unit has proposed that a more accurate measure of unemployment is provided by the approach recommended by the International Labour Office and the Organisation for Economic Co-operation and Development. In effect, this means that the unemployed are defined as those who did not undertake more than one hour's work for pay or profit during the week prior to interview, who actively sought work during the four weeks prior to interview, and who were free to begin a job within a fortnight. In addition, however, the ILO recommend the inclusion of certain 'discouraged' workers, that is people who did not look for work in the relevant period because local labour market conditions make this pointless.[10]

But even this underestimates the magnitude of the problem because of the effects on the numbers of the government's 'special employment measures'. These include the numerous 'training' schemes, Action for Community Employment, the Enterprise Allowance Scheme etc., discussed in more detail later on in this report. If we start thinking in terms of the number of jobs which need to be developed to provide work for everyone who wants work in West Belfast—what is usually referred to as 'the jobs gap'—it is clear that the official unemployment figures are not much help. We estimate that the true jobs gap in West Belfast is well over 18,000.

Over the last year or so the British government has been celebrating an apparent downward trend in unemployment. It is almost as if the problem is solved. Most of the drop in the figures, however, has nothing to do with any supposed up-turn in the economy or with an expansion in employment. Table 6.5 shows that during 1987, unemployment in the North of Ireland went down by 7,767, according to the official figures. This decline was not matched, however, by a corresponding increase in jobs over the same period. In fact the number of male employees *went down* by 1,120 and although the number of females in employment rose by 2,850, this cannot account for the full decline in unemployment numbers.

Table 6.5: *Changes in Numbers Working and Unemployed between 1986 and 1987 (seasonally adjusted).*[11]

	MALES	FEMALES	TOTAL
Unemployed Dec. 1986	92,621	33,836	126,457
Unemployed Dec. 1987	87,517	31,173	118,690
Change in Unemployed 1986-7	−5,105	−2,663	−7,767
Change in Employees in Employment 1986-7	−1,120	+2,850	+1,730
Change in Total Working Population 1986-7			−5,501

On the basis of the broader measure of 'total working population' the figures look even worse with an overall decline of 5,501. Some of the 'missing' unemployed will of course have been absorbed by training schemes. Perhaps this is why such trainees will soon be regarded as 'in employment' according to official definitions. McCullagh's conclusion seems entirely fitting in the light of this statistical history:

> 'Official unemployment statistics should be viewed ... as the end product of a social process of negotiation and struggle between various social groups which were (and are) seeking to establish their claim to the status of officially unemployed. The state has played a central role in mediating this process and in conferring legitimacy on the unemployment status of some groups.'[12]

Personal Consequences

One outcome of economic recession is a certain amount of work for social researchers investigating what unemployment does to people. Studies of the effects of recession in Europe and the US in the 1930s gave rise to the notion that people go through a series of stages as they adjust to being unemployed. When they first hear that they will be out of work, there is shock and disbelief. This is followed by a short period of optimism and confidence in their ability to find work again. But as time goes on, the mood changes to one of growing insecurity and self-doubt. The final stage, characterised by apathy and boredom, is one in which the unemployed person becomes reconciled to their situation.

During the current recession, this stages model has been attacked for its failure to recognise the diversity of responses to unemployment and its lack of attention to ill-health. Too often in the past, researchers concentrated their attentions on men with families who had been in regular manufacturing employment for some years. It was this *specific* situation that had come to dominate accounts of responses to unemployment.[13]

Contemporary studies make it clear that how unemployment effects people depends very much on their previous experiences of work (if any), their expectations, the value they place on work as a source of self-esteem, and the extent to which their lives are dominated and structured by paid work as an activity. In all of this, much will depend on the unemployed person's class, their stage in the life cycle, and whether they are a woman or a man.[14]

Nevertheless, it is widely reported that certain negative responses are so pervasive that some key generalisations can be made. Regarding research in the North, studies by Evason and Trew and Kilpatrick both emphasized psychological deterioration and boredom, as well as loss of health.[15] Depression was commonly reported in both studies and this finding was substantiated by one West Belfast GP we interviewed. There now seems little doubt that unemployment damages health and in some cases leads to premature death through heart problems and sometimes through suicide.[16]

Unemployment is also related to the incidence of marital strain and domestic violence, although this is not to say that unemployment *causes* these things. It is, though, reported to exacerbate tensions within households. Two significant findings from Evason's Derry study were that over three-quarters of the sample reported that unemployment was having a negative effect on their marriage, and over 40% stated that their children were unable to participate in school trips or outings because of lack of money.

Another significant finding was that Protestants were much more likely than Catholics to report loss of self-esteem and confidence as a result of unemployment. None of the sample could be described as having gained immunity from anxiety and a sense of demoralisation which accompanies unemployment, yet there were noticeable differences in relation to self-respect. Howe's study mentioned in Chapter 4 suggests this stems from the different position and experience of Catholics and Protestants in relation to the economy. It may also be the product of different political perceptions and responses.

Unemployment may effect the self image of Protestants and Catholics differently, but this does not mean that the latter escape from the social consequences of unemployment. A number of professional workers based in West Belfast told us that people in the area, especially young people, had become used to unemployment in the sense that *they expected never to have work*. This lack of expectations stems from the experience of parents, brothers and sisters who have rarely been in employment, and is particularly prevalent in heavily stigmatised estates such as Divis. Low expectations pose many problems, particularly in relation to young people and anti-social behaviour. A hidden economy based on petty theft and burglary, and the exchange of stolen goods has emerged, providing young people with virtually the only source of ready cash and means of escape from the sense of hopelessness which has pervaded their upbringing. This is not to excuse such anti-social activities, but it is to say that long-term exclusion from work helps to explain what one probation officer described as 'the absence of the normal structures that create routines, boundaries and rules'.

High levels of unemployment have a deeply corrosive effect on the daily lives of the unemployed and the communities in which they live. Some of the effects are visible and self-evidently destructive. But frequently the effects are suffered privately in silence behind closed doors. Nevertheless, the research suggests that the unemployed do not blame themselves for their predicament. Most have a clear perception of what causes the problem: three-quarters of Evason's sample said responsibility lay with 'Mrs. Thatcher', 'the government' or 'the recession'. Less than 10% blamed themselves in terms of ill-health or other problems, and only a handful blamed 'the troubles'. Similarly, Trew and Kilpatrick showed that unemployed men in Belfast were coping significantly better with the psychological stresses of unemployment than a sample drawn from Brighton. They explain this in terms of the high levels of communal solidarity in Belfast, reflecting the long-term and extreme nature of the unemployment problem and the support provided by close family networks. The evidence suggests, therefore, that while the North's unemployed suffer the usual ill-effects of unemployment, they retain a political perception of the problem and are less psychologically demoralized than might be expected.

Footnotes

1. Compiled from DED statistics.
2. Compiled from DED statistics.

3. Falls Community Council, *West Belfast, Some of the Facts behind the Issues* and Community Research Services, *A Social and Economic Profile of the Households in the Lower Shankill*, Belfast: Centre for the Unemployed, 1988.
4. *Unemployment Bulletins* Nos. 18, 20, 21, 24 and 25.
5. Hansard WA 10/12/86 cols. 155-6.
6. *Independent* 15/7/88.
7. Hansard WA 8/4/87 cols. 329-32.
8. *Unemployment Bulletin* No. 26, Spring 1988, p. 6.
9. *Observer* 29/11/87.
10. *Unemployment Bulletin* No. 26, Spring 1988, p. 9.
11. Compiled from DED figures. Note: since compiling this table, figures have been released which show the total working population to have expanded recently. This does not alter the point that the 'unemployment decline' cannot be accounted for by a claimed growth in jobs.
12. McCullagh, M., 'The Social Construction of Unemployment', in Clancy, P. *et al* (eds.), *Ireland: A Sociological Profile*. Dublin: Institute of Public Administration, 1986, p. 312.
13. For a review of research prior to 1982, see Kelvin, P. and Jarrett, J., *Unemployment: Its Social Psychological Effects*, Cambridge: Cambridge University Press, 1985.
14. See for example the findings in Allen, S. *et al* (eds.), *The Experience of Unemployment*, London: Macmillan, 1986.
15. Evason, E., *On the Edge: a study of poverty and long-term unemployment in Northern Ireland*, London: Child Poverty Action Group, 1985, and Trew, K. and Kilpatrick, R., *The Daily Life of the Unemployed*, Belfast: Queen's University, 1984.
16. The best summary of the arguments and evidence about unemployment and ill-health is Richard Smith's book, *Unemployment and Health: A Disaster and a Challenge*, Oxford: Oxford University Press, 1987. In relation specifically to suicide, a committee of independent health experts under the chairpersonship of Professor Alwyn Smith, produced in 1988 what they claimed to be the first comprehensive review of the state of people's health in Britain. In it they concluded that the suicide rate of the unemployed was twice the national average. See *The Nation's Health*, London: King Edward's Hospital Fund for London, 1988.

7.

Economic Development Policy: The IDB, LEDU and West Belfast

Unionism and Job Creation

From 1945 the Northern Ireland government followed a policy of intervening in the economy to encourage and support enterprise and job creation whether locally based or resulting from foreign investment. Admittedly such a policy was half-heartedly pursued by what was, after all, a party which was not only Unionist but also highly conservative. The lack of enthusiasm was increasingly criticised in the mid-1950s by economists, business people, trade unionists and church leaders, resulting in the Unionist government eventually relenting to produce a package of incentives specifically designed to entice foreign capital. Throughout the 1960s and 1970s this package was expanded, to the point where it became, in the words of Secretary of State Roy Mason, 'one of the best in Western Europe'.

The strategy had some success. The multinationals came to invest, especially in the area of synthetic fibre production. By 1976 one fifth of all the synthetic fibre production in the UK took place in the North.[1] This was ironic, given that the global growth of synthetics had been a major cause of the decline of one of the North's two staple industries, linen production. Yet, by the 1960s and 1970s synthetics had become the partial saviour of the North's economy. Such production could not hope to reverse the North's economic decline, but for a while it did much to slow it down.

The policy of enticing multinationals seemed to be a success story. Beneath the surface, however, there were major problems. In line with policies in Britain and elsewhere at the time, a regional plan was drawn up for the North in the mid-1960s. This Matthew Plan proposed that new investment be encouraged to settle outside Belfast. In effect, a zone of development was designated taking in such areas as Antrim/Ballymena and Lurgan/Portadown. Not only did this plan succeed in speeding up the decline, economic and otherwise, of Belfast, but it became in effect sectarian. As Catholic women lost their jobs in the mills of West Belfast, Protestant men acquired the new jobs in the newly designated growth centres. Majority Catholic towns like Derry and Strabane, which by any measure of deprivation deserved to have investment pushed their direction, fared badly, while Protestant towns like Carrickfergus, Larne, Antrim, Ballymena, Coleraine, Bangor, Lurgan and Portadown (with the 'orange elephant' of Craigavon in between) thrived.

Belfast as a whole benefited little from the regional development strategy. The city itself, and in particular the inner city, rapidly declined as new factories were pushed towards the suburbs of Newtownabbey in the north and Castlereagh and Dundonald in the east. West Belfast fared worst of all. According to unpublished government records, between 1946 and June 1980, 180 companies from outside Northern Ireland were given state aid to establish in the North. Of those, three located in West Belfast. The first, Ford Autolite, was established in 1964, almost 20 years after the state economic intervention strategy began. It was another 15 years before the next two firms, Fisher Body and American Monitor, arrived in West Belfast.

Northern Ireland-based firms in West Belfast benefited little from the increasingly supportive state policies. As far as can be ascertained, between 1945 and 1971 only one such firm received any government economic assistance—Macrete on the Andersonstown Road. (Prior to 1945 Mackies received a little state aid.)

Direct Rule

The renewed British interest in Irish affairs as a result of the events of 1969 led quickly to the relegation of local government. Overwhelmingly sectarian councils lost most of their powers to non-elected Health and Social Services Area Boards, Education and Library Boards and the Housing Executive, all of which became responsible to government departments at Stormont.[2] With the establishment of direct rule in 1972, the power of these departments increased dramatically. To all intents and purposes the cluster of departments under the Northern Ireland Office (NIO) became a massive, powerful and relatively unaccountable monolith. Not only had they the same powers as similar central government Departments in Britain, but they also had the ultimate responsiblity for funding and controlling those functions taken away from local government. In addition, in an economy where 40% of jobs are directly dependent on the state and at least a further 20% indirectly state-dependent, the power of government departments as employer, paymaster and judge was unrivalled in Western Europe.

One of the most powerful Departments is the one which, after a number of reshufflings, mergers and name changes, became known in the early 1980s as the Department of Economic Development—the DED. Under its wing is responsibility for encouraging foreign investment, supporting locally-based enterprises, job training, youth employment schemes, Action for Community Employment (ACE), etc. The Industrial Development Board (IDB), which has an expenditure of approximately £100m per year, and the Local Enterprise Development Unit (LEDU), whose annual budget is in the region of £25m, are both DED minions.

The regroupment of the Stormont ministries in the 1970s coincided with a partial awareness that the regional strategy had served to speed up the decline of Belfast, leaving its economic base on the edge of collapse. Numerous reports spelt out the details of Belfast's illness. One response was to encourage firms to establish in Belfast and, once established, to support them through rough periods. This partial reversal of economic strategy led to West Belfast acquiring new jobs on a scale unprecedented in this century—D.C. Products in 1974, Antrim Crystal in 1975, Strathearn Audio in 1977, Fisher Body and American Monitor in 1979. Most of these were in the Kennedy Way Industrial Estate, built in 1974 and representing the first move by government to establish such an industrial estate in West Belfast itself. Previously the closest such estates had been to West Belfast was Dunmurry, in the neighbouring Lisburn District Council area.

But the flagship of government claims to be doing something about unemployment in West Belfast was the De Lorean Motor Company. Although not based in West Belfast nor, for that matter, employing people exclusively from the area, its proposed target of 2,500 jobs by the early 1980s meant that the factory's establishment in Dunmurry in 1978 was greeted with the sort of fanfares not heard in Belfast since the launch of the Titanic. As it turned out, De Lorean sank as surely as did the Titanic, and almost as quickly.

In retrospect, it is clear that there were hints in the very establishment of the De Lorean venture of harsher economic times to come.[3] By the late 1970s the world recession was beginning to take effect. There was little in the way of footloose capital running around the globe looking for somewhere to nest and therefore open to enticement to the North. De Lorean was wooed by the NIO after his plans for a sports car factory had been rejected by investors and governments in the US, Puerto Rico and the South of Ireland. It quickly became apparent that West Belfast had got the scrapings of the barrel. De Lorean closed within three years of opening.

The recession of the 1980s ripped apart any gains of the regional strategy of the previous three decades. Its effects on the North's economy can be seen in three areas. Firstly, the multinationals regrouped, sacrificing peripheral European operations, even those that were financially successful, in the interests of re-establishing elsewhere, particularly in the Third World. Most spectacularly, the synthetic fibres giants toppled in quick succession, throwing tens of thousands onto the dole. In 1981 alone such closures led to over 20,000 jobs being lost.[4] Secondly, because of rationalisation and regroupment on the part of multinational companies there was less excess global investment seeking a home and therefore susceptible to NIO claims about the value of their economic incentives. Furthermore, what investment there was, as already noted, was heading to Third World nations, with Third World wages, health and safety conditions and trade union organisation. It could not easily be persuaded to head to Northern Ireland except by the ploy of reducing workers here to the vulnerable and exploitable levels of Third World workers. Thirdly, increased competition between multinational firms as the recession bit led to mergers, takeovers and straightforward steamrolling of larger giants over smaller companies.

Figure 7.1

Summary of Major Closures in or near West Belfast

DATE	COMPANY	JOB LOSS	
1976	Ewart's Mill (Crumlin Rd.)	1,340	(since 1968)
1976	Falls Flax (Cupar St.)	370	(since 1969)
1978	Carrington Viyella	400	
1978	Ladybird Clothing	200	
1979	Peter Pan Bakery	500	
1980	Antrim Crystal	140	
1980	Lucozade	70	
1980	Strathearn Audio	260	(since 1977)
1981	Falls Flax (Conway St.)	206	(since 1969)
1981	Grundig	1,030	
1982	De Lorean	1,500	
1985	American Monitor	120	(since 1983)
1987	Brough, Cox and Dunn	30	
1988	Eastwoods	?	

N.B. *James Mackie and Sons Ltd* employed 4,500 workers in the 1960s, the vast majority from the Shankill. By 1980 the workforce was down to 2,400. In 1981 a further 720 redundancies were announced, followed by 400 more in 1982.

The total losses (including Mackies) amount to 9,400.

Like the growth centres outside Belfast, West Belfast experienced these effects of the recession. However, in West Belfast's case the effects were particularly ironic given that the area had only recently begun to gain any benefits from state economic intervention. Firstly, multinational regroupment led to the closing down of places of employment in or near West Belfast (see Figure 7.1 for a list of recent closures in the area and Figure 7.2 for the details of the closure of American Monitor in 1985). Secondly, while some new investment may have continued to trickle into Northern Ireland, it was diverted to places like Newtownabbey and Ballymena—none of it reached West Belfast. In addition, West Belfast had the bad image of the De Lorean failure to contend with. There was no way that a monetarist Tory government with Secretaries of State lacking in the bravado and arrogance of

Labour's Roy Mason was going to 'do another De Lorean',[5] even though it was clear that the failure of that experiment had nothing to do with the quality or eagerness of the workers in West Belfast. Thirdly, increased competition meant that even viable West Belfast firms—like Lucozade (see Figure 7.3) and Peter Pan Bakeries (see Figure 7.4)—were swamped in the struggle of larger companies.

Figure 7.2

American Monitor International Ltd.
Kennedy Way Industrial Estate

Thirty-two people lost their jobs with the closure of American Monitor in January 1985. The factory was set up in 1980 by the Northern Ireland Development Agency to manufacture blood testing equipment. American Monitor initially said that its eventual jobs target would be 250 over a three year period.

The company however was forced into difficulties by increasingly sophisticated European production cutting into its markets. The high cost of the Belfast equipment made it hard to sell at a time of increasing financial stringency for medical centres. (The cost of each item produced was £250,000.)

The jobs target of 250 was never achieved with the workforce peak rising to just 120 towards the end of 1983.

Staff levels were consistently cut by management in an effort to trim costs with substantial pay-offs taking place in November 1984, leaving the firm with a minimum workforce.

In 1984, the parent company in Indianapolis decided that the Kennedy Way plant would become a component and sub-assembly source for instruments made in America.

Other financial interests in the company were as follows:

The Industrial Development Board held a 23% stake in American Monitor PLC , the company formed in 1983 after a radical attempt to re-finance the firm. The Legal and General Insurance Company was the largest of the private investors, with the rest of the shares owned by American Monitor.

The actual liquidation decision was taken due to 'continuing difficulties caused by cash flow problems and increasing difficulties facing the parent company, American Monitor Corporation.' The latter corporation filed for protection against creditors under United States bankruptcy laws.

Referring to the closure, the then Industry Minister, Rhodes Boyson, said the closure was a bitter blow to the West Belfast area:

> 'The IDB has been closely involved with the company, but unfortunately the American parent company has experienced severe cash flow problems. It is regrettable that despite significant financial assistance to the local company from both the private and the public sector it has been impossible to prevent closure.'

Figure 7.3

Lucozade Factory, Andersonstown Road

The Lucozade factory in Andersonstown closed in May 1980 after nearly 30 years in production. Seventy jobs were lost.

Local management were summoned to the firm's head office in London in March 1980 where they were told that the Andersonstown plant was no longer economically viable because of the high cost of serving such a small area as the North. The cost of doing so was far out of proportion with costs in England and Scotland where more people were served with 'less mileage'.

Following the closure, Lucozade products were distributed throughout the North by Williames Transport.

Lucozade is owned by Beechams, the multinational which owns Macleans Toothpaste and Brylcream among other products.

Figure 7.4

Peter Pan Bakery, Springfield Road

The Peter Pan Bakery closed in June 1979 throwing over 400 people out of work. Peter Pan was then the biggest employer of nationalist working class people in West Belfast.

The Peter Pan Bakery was formed in 1974 as a merger of two Belfast firms, Hughes' and Kennedy's and the Derry firm of Eaton's. The 1974 merger was an attempt by the three firms to join together to prevent themselves being put out of business by the larger bread manufacturing firms. The giants in the market in the North at the time were two British firms, Associated British Foods (ABF) and Rank Hovis McDougall (RHM) who dominated the market through their local representatives, Sunblest and Milanda.

These two major British concerns tried to squeeze their Belfast-based rivals, Peter Pan and Ormo, out of the market through maintaining artificially low bread prices. This involved a short-term cut in profits for ABF and RHM, a loss which the large British firms could absorb, in order to gain the longer-term benefits of driving their Belfast competitors out of business. Once the Belfast bakeries were out of business, the large firms could then raise bread prices in unison, government policies permitting.

In 1974, the year of Peter Pan's formation, the Gibson Report was published which surveyed the North's bakery industry for the British government. Gibson maintained that the bakeries were over-producing here by some 20% and proposed that one major bakery should close to provide a healthy market for the rest. The proposals underlined the economic process which would establish the total dominance of the giants ABF and RHM. Gibson recommended that directors of firms closing voluntarily should be paid inflated prices for their shares and that posts should be found for them elsewhere, whilst the workers should receive double redundancy pay. These measres were proposed to sweeten the bitter pill of closure and redundancy and thus speed up the process of rationalization in the bakery industry.

Gibson's proposals were accepted by the then British Labour government who offered Peter Pan a golden handshake of £1½ million, to be shared between the management and workers if they closed and secured the market for other bakeries. But the plan was rejected by the management of Peter Pan who attempted to hold on to their 17% share of the bread market, despite being financially weak.

In order to compete and maintain their profit level, Peter Pan's management reduced their workforce each year after 1974. In one year, fifty men were sacked, though the remaining workforce were required to maintain the previous level of production, thus ensuring that sales were maintained while costs were cut.

In June 1978, their profit level again falling, the directors of Peter Pan met representatives of the British government to demand an increase in the government-controlled price of bread. Instead the British government resurrected Gibson's 1974 proposals for those firms prepared to voluntarily close down. The Directors accepted these proposals as a last resort, believing they had no option but to close without an injection of capital into the company. They began to run down the firm without informing the workforce.

The company was an estimated £500,000 in debt and both management and unions requested £2 million in aid from the British government in the form of a Temporary Employment Subsidy. In March 1979, the company received a miserly £30,000 in Temporary Employment Subsidy and the British government refused to permit an increase in the price of bread.

The management conceded that the company would go out of business and informed the unions that the business was to be bought over by three other firms—Allied, Milanda and Ormo.

When the workers learned in January 1979 that the firm was due to go out of business they investigated the possibility of keeping the bakery open by running it as a co-operative. At the early stages of their investigations, the proposition looked promising until the workers learned that the firm owed £1 million to suppliers of materials. The idea of continuing the bakery as a co-operative had to be shelved due to the problem of starting out with the financial burden of debt. The workers did approach the government for financial assistance but failed to get any.

The bakery workers started a campaign in West Belfast, calling on people to buy Peter Pan bread. It was hoped that a rise in the demand for Peter Pan bread might secure their jobs. However, their efforts were unsuccessful and the firm closed in June 1979. Of the 500 workers at Peter Pan who were made redundant, about 100 managed to find work in other bakeries.

Up until the beginning of April 1979, there had been high hopes that, if the Department of Commerce were not prepared to underwrite the firm's debt, that they would at least 'sugar the pill' by granting a double redundancy scheme, whereby the workers would receive 13 weeks pay in lieu of notice on top of the usual redundancy. But with the change in government, and a consequent hardening of attitudes, the scheme went by the board. This in fact meant that the workers were deprived of approximately £800 each when the firm closed.

The effects of the recession led to changes in the DED's role. Inevitably, it moved to a more defensive strategy—bailing out firms in economic difficulty through grants, partial acquisition of the companies' shares, etc. But even this defensive role had its limits within a general government policy that market forces should prevail.[6] Given that, the DED's defence of ailing firms in West Belfast was frequently less than could have been expected for an area with so few sources of employment for redundant local workers to fall back on. The DED's record in attempting to save American Monitor (which led it to purchase 2 million £1 shares, 2 million 10p shares and almost 3 million 40p shares in the company) would seem to be laudable. But employees and unions in Strathearn (100% government owned and the victim of poor management and unexpectably stiff competition from the Japanese audio equipment manufacturing industry)[7] and Peter Pan (locally owned, but forced to close because of intense competition from British conglomerates) argued that the government could have done more to save otherwise viable firms.

Of course, the DED did not abandon its offensive role altogether. In fact, in an attempt to counter media images of violence, its own image became glossier and more flamboyant. Yet, it is clear that its continuing, though severely decreased, success in enticing foreign investment did little to benefit West Belfast. Even the introduction of differential grant aid for capital projects in areas of high unemployment did not prove attractive to foreign firms. When they could get 40% capital grant aid to establish in any other area of the North, and only 50% to establish in areas such as West Belfast, the differential was not big enough to persuade them to abandon areas of proven economic success. It would seem that the DED succeeded in doing little to persuade them to try other, less spectacular areas.

All in all the DED's role in job creation and job protection in West Belfast has not shown inspiring results. This is evident in considering the record of two of its main job creation instruments, the IDB and LEDU.

The Industrial Development Board

The IDB is the 'big gun' of government job creation policy. Its apparently limitless budget and its wide brief mean that few firms of any size in the North, whether locally owned or not, avoid dealing with it at some point or other in their existence. However, the IDB's efforts have done remarkably little to revive West Belfast's economy.

The IDB has two major functions. Firstly, it provides economic assistance to new or already existing firms. Such assistance includes capital grants, employment grants, rent grants and interest relief grants. Secondly, the IDB can buy shares in a company. It does this usually as part of its rescue function. In short, IDB ownership of a company's shares is one of the surest signs that the company is in severe economic difficulties.

An examination of the last three annual reports of the IDB gives some sense of how West Belfast has fared in relation to the IDB's first function, grant aid. The total assistance to firms in West Belfast in the financial years 1984/5 and 1985/6 is as follows:[8]

Clarence Clothing Company	£81,000 (1984/5)
Eastwood's	£62,000 (1984/5)
Ford Motor Company	£1,236,000 (1985/6)

giving a total of £1,379,000. In those same two years the IDB paid out £126,130,000 to firms throughout the North. In short, West Belfast's economic assistance amounted to 1% of the total budget in grant aid in those two financial years.[9]

To first appearances West Belfast benefited much more from the IDB's second function. In 1984/5 the IDB owned 11,941,042 shares in 36 separate companies. A massive amount of those shares, 6,746,049—56.5%—were in one company, the West Belfast-based American Monitor. A similar situation prevailed in 1985/6, with American Monitor accounting for 57.3% of IDB's total share holdings. However, the actual amounts involved in share holding in relation to the IDB's total budget are not particularly large. Because the companies are already in difficulty when the IDB intervenes, the actual financial value of the shares at the point of IDB purchase is in fact low. It is impossible to determine from annual reports what was the actual financial stake of the IDB through share purchase in each company; for example, in 1985/6 did the 195,000 £1 shares the IDB owned in Trimtech Ltd cost more or less in straight monetary terms than the 49,000 £1 shares in CP Trim Ltd? Only the IDB can answer that. But what can be said is that *all* share holding by the IDB in 1985/6 came to £1,520,000—in that same year the IDB loaned £7,005,000, gave £74,447,000 in grant aid, allocated £9,552,000 to factory building, and so on. The proportion of shares owned in one West Belfast company, large as that proportion was, has to be seen in the context of everything else that the IDB did with its money, and where it did it. To underline that context: the IDB spent £1,317,000 on the maintenance of the estates it already owned in 1985/6, an amount almost equal to what it spent on share acquisition in 35 ailing companies, American Monitor included.

More importantly, it must be remembered that share purchase is often a last ditch effort. Companies which become the focus of such special attention frequently do not survive. American Monitor is a clear example. After its collapse the IDB only allocated £440,000 to share holding in 1986/7, giving it a stake of 3,653,850 shares in 30 separate companies. Only one of these, Brough, Cox and Dunn, since deceased, was in the West Belfast constituency. Again, while no estimate can be made on the basis of published annual reports of the actual amount of money involved in buying 100,000 shares in Brough, Cox and Dunn, the fact is clear that IDB share ownership in West Belfast in 1986/7 was 2.7% of its total share ownership in that year.

West Belfast will not account for such a large proportion of the IDB's ownership of shares as it did in 1984/5 and 1985/6 unless and until a firm of the size of American Monitor is close to collapse. Given the lack of such firms in the area, it is in other areas that IDB will focus its rescue function. In that sense, the unsuccessful attempt to save American Monitor typifies perfectly the IDB's approach to West Belfast—a very low level of grant aid, punctuated infrequently by relatively spectacular but ultimately unsuccessful rescue attempts.

What is clear above all is that the IDB does not regard it as one of its functions to take affirmative action on behalf of areas of high unemployment. It responds to market demands, whether that means providing factories for Japanese firms in Newtownabbey and Ballymena because that is where the Japanese want to locate, or rushing to the aid of firms collapsing under the pressure of market forces. The identification of areas of need in relation to job creation is not part of IDB logic. If it were, the organisation would be involved in drawing up definite plans to channel investment to such areas and would be doing everything possible to pre-empt the need for stepping in at the last minute as a sort of financial fire brigade.

Local Enterprise Development Unit

LEDU exists to encourage the establishment of small businesses. It has had a successful record over the last decade in sponsoring jobs. Moreover, the LEDU strategy is much cheaper than that of the IDB, producing jobs at the cost of £6,250 per job, compared to the IDB average of £23,500 for each job resulting from inward investment.[10]

As such, LEDU fits neatly into the current British government argument that economic revival must derive much more from local effort than from government support, that is, from the creation of a vibrant local 'enterprise culture'. But it is patently obvious that LEDU, which promoted 4,244 jobs in 1987 (the IDB promoted 4,187 jobs in 1986/7, with a further 8,515 jobs 'renewed and maintained') cannot single-handedly revive the North's moribund economy. The very best that can be hoped for is that it plays its role in tandem with other endeavours.

But there are further criticisms which can be made of LEDU in the context of West Belfast. Unlike the IDB, which up until recently produced lists of firms assisted and amounts given to each of them in its annual reports, LEDU is highly protective of its information. It does reveal how many jobs it creates each year in the Greater Belfast area, but no more detailed breakdown of help specifically to West Belfast is available. Despite the lack of detailed information, it would appear that for many years LEDU, like its 'big brother', the IDB, did not prioritise West Belfast, nor produce any blueprint for affirmative action in job creation for the area. Part of the reason for this is LEDU's (and the IDB's) unwillingness to undertake such a directive and interventionist role, preferring instead to react to requests for help from local enterprises. This policy is problematic in the case of areas of high unemployment like West Belfast.

Firstly, given the relative lack of local enterprises and indeed of local capital, LEDU's reactive policy means that more help is given to areas which are already economically stronger than West Belfast.

But a more significant restriction on LEDU's operations is the fact that its hands are in effect tied as a result of politico/economic policies emanating from elsewhere. Certain requests for help are less legitimate than others. A prime example of this is in relation to a comparison of the Conway Mill on the Falls Road and Brookfield Mill in Ardoyne, North Belfast. Both are enterprises based in derelict mills, both are within the Enterprise Zone and therefore eligible for derating, cutting of red tape and other economic incentives, and both are managed by local priests. Brookfield Mill is said to epitomise what local endeavour can achieve—a successful transformation of the derelict mill into a site for small industrial and distributive units, training and, perhaps most imaginatively of all, an incubation unit where people with a business idea judged to be sound are given maximum backing for one year to establish their project. Despite the highlighting of local enterprise, Brookfield Mill's success depends heavily on government local intervention—albeit masked under various schemes ranging from ACE to YTP, and from the Urban Development Grant scheme to LEDU assistance. Conversely, the underdevelopment of the Conway Mill does not result from a lack of local enterprise, but from an equally sustained intervention on the part of government to block the development of the project. The reason for the stark difference between the two projects will be spelt out in Chapter 10. Suffice it to say here that the NIO's unproven belief that the Conway Mill is a front for paramilitary interests through which, consequently, public funds are being siphoned off to 'terrorists' is at the root of the government's discriminatory action. In this regard the NIO is involved in what might be called 'the politics of example'.

Brookfield is held up for all as the epitome of 'respectable community-based' initiative, that is, based on self-help and not involving anyone whom the government judges to be a fellow-traveller of paramilitaries. The Conway Mill is presented as the archetypal example of a 'non-respectable' community initiative and therefore does not receive financial backing.

As an arm of government economic development policy, LEDU is unable to act independently of government guidelines, even if it wanted to. It cannot, for example, decide that the Conway Mill project is worth backing on the basis of merit, but must follow the three line whip of the NIO on this matter. Chapter 10 spells out the details of how it has in fact done so in relation to the Conway Mill.

Figure 7.5

'Ulster Development Boss Accused of Jobs Bias'
Guardian **23/9/87**

In September 1987 Eddie McGrady, SDLP MP for South Down, asked the NIO to review the appointment of Mervyn Hadden as chairperson of LEDU. Hadden is also chairperson of Aircraft Furnishing in Kilkeel, Co. Down. His company has had a number of successes recently in terms of attracting orders, including a £5m contract from British Airways to provide lightweight seats for aeroplanes. Consequently, the workforce at the factory has been expanded by 51 to 247 employees. However, as McGrady pointed out, only eight of the new recruits were Catholic, even though the area in which the factory is situated is predominantly Catholic. In one instance a skilled worker, a Catholic, was unsuccessful with Aircraft Furnishing, but later got a job at Shorts, while an unskilled Protestant was successful when he applied for a job at Aircraft Furnishing.

Recently LEDU has begun to show signs of increased activity in relation to West Belfast, not because it has changed its strategy and decided to take a more directive role, but because the political issue of unemployment in West Belfast has led to a proliferation of schemes and plans, such as the West Belfast Development Trust and the Townsend Enterprise Park. Backed by the combined forces of the Catholic church, professionals with links to West Belfast and local constitutionalist Nationalists, such current schemes, like the Brookfield Mill before them, fit neatly into government strategy. They become eminently suitable for LEDU and other backing. This is not to say that the schemes have no merit. It is to conclude, however, that merit is not the sole criterion of assistance. There is no way that these groups can be accused by the NIO of being paramilitary fronts and this, together with a judgement about the viability of the projects concerned, becomes the basis for financial backing.

In short, there has been a sudden upsurge in the number of groups in West Belfast seeking assistance for economic development projects which, under NIO guidelines, are eligible for such assistance. Given the nature of the resources available to such groups, they are not attempting to set up branch plants of large multinational corporations, but are gearing their efforts towards smaller, more localised business enterprises. Such groups thus come in contact with LEDU rather than the IDB, both of which are by design sitting waiting for such approaches. Thus it is LEDU which, apart from having an increasing role in West Belfast in terms of economic development, has also become in effect an economic weapon for political ends. LEDU is an important channel by which the power of the DED reaches into the heart of the community.

Footnotes

1. Quigley Report, *Economic and Industrial Strategy for Northern Ireland: Report of a Review Team*, Belfast 1976: 53; cited in O'Dowd, L., 'Regional Policy', in L. O'Dowd, B. Rolston and M. Tomlinson, *Northern Ireland: Between Civil Rights and Civil War*, London, CSE Books, 1980: p. 53.
2. See Tomlinson, M., 'Relegating Local Government', in L. O'Dowd, *et al, op. cit*: pp. 95-118.
3. See 'De Lorean: The Facts Behind the Bullshit', *Belfast Bulletin* 5, 1979: pp. 41-48.
4. See 'A Year of Collapse', *Belfast Bulletin* 10, 1982: pp. 81-3.
5. Thus Ian Paisley, among others, criticised the excessive caution of the NIO in failing to back a sports car project in 1983. A Northampton company, Automotive Designs, sought £600,000 from government to set up a plant to produce a two seater sports car called the Charisma. They envisaged a workforce of 80 producing initially 100 cars per year. Paisley quoted an IDB letter to Automotive Designs which, in a reference to the De Lorean fiasco, contained the admission that they were 'once bitten, twice shy' (*Belfast Telegraph* 8/3/83).
6. Before recent speculation of privatisation, the Harland and Wolff shipyard proved the most important exception to this rule. One reason for this has been the unwillingness to suffer the political consequences of closing down such a major site of skilled Protestant employment, a point made by Secretary of State Jim Prior when he spoke, in a code that Belfast residents could well understand, of his reluctance to close the Yard because it stood as a 'symbol of industrial Belfast' (NIO Press Release, 12/5/82).
7. See 'The Great Strathearn Rip-Off', *Belfast Bulletin* 4, 1978: pp. 21-6.
8. Interestingly, for the first time no breakdown of specific firms receiving grant aid was given in the Annual Report for 1986/7.
9. Further evidence on the relative unimportance of West Belfast is provided by the fact that not one of the 'high fliers' chosen for special mention in the IDB's annual report for 1986/7 is in West Belfast.
10. *Economic Strategy: Industrial Development*, Northern Ireland Economic Council Report Number 60, August 1986, p. 14.

8.

International Aid and West Belfast

Introduction

In recent years aid for economic disaster areas such as West Belfast has not been confined to funds available directly from government Departments. In the last decade the importance of the European Community, and particularly its Social Fund and Regional Development Fund have operated supposedly to redistribute funds from the richer to the poorer parts of Europe. As far as the EEC is concerned, the North of Ireland is one of the two poorest parts of Europe, the other being Calabria in Italy. Within the North, as we have shown, West Belfast ranks as one of the poorest areas. Consequently, the amount of EEC finances reaching West Belfast is a measure of whether or not the logic of redistribution actually works. It is the argument of this chapter that West Belfast has not gained greatly from EEC funding. The reason for this, we argue, is that the purse strings are controlled by the same government Departments which, as the previous chapter has shown, have a woeful record in terms of countering the social problems of West Belfast.

The EEC is supposedly independent of such local bodies as the Department of Economic Development. But the fact that the EEC has left the administration of its funding to the North in the hands of such bodies has meant that the distribution of funds is subject to the criteria and shortcomings of government Departments. The same conclusion can be reached in relation to a more recent arrival on the scene of international aid to the North, the International Fund for Ireland, set up as a result of the Hillsborough Agreement of November 1985. This chapter also considers the failure of that Fund's operations to lead to the economic reconstruction of West Belfast.

The International Fund for Ireland

Since the signing of the Hillsborough Agreement in November 1985, there has existed the International Fund for Ireland, a pool of money mainly from the US (but also from Canada, New Zealand and most recently the EEC) to 'promote peace and reconciliation through economic and social advances' in the North as well as Donegal, Cavan,

Monaghan, Sligo, Leitrim and Louth. To date the Fund has channelled significant sums of money to the general West Belfast area (a larger area than the constituency) as Table 8.1 shows.

Table 8.1: *The West Belfast Area and International Fund Aid.*

Townsend Enterprise Park	£250,000
Farset Enterprises	£180,000
West Link Enterprises	£160,000
West Belfast Development Trust	£160,000
Glenwood Enterprises Ltd	£150,000
Action Resource Centre	£75,000
Phoenix Development Trust	£50,000

After its most recent announcement of allocation (which included £400,000 towards the building of a new hotel in the centre of Belfast and £200,000 for medical research at the Royal Hospital), SDLP MP Seamus Mallon complained that, although he had expected that the value of the International Fund would be that it would bring 'help and hope to those areas which have suffered most', it was instead concentrating 'its efforts and other people's money on servicing big business'.[2] The Fund's governing board were quick to reply to Mallon, rejecting his allegations and pointing out that priority was given to all areas of particular disadvantage, including West and North Belfast and Derry.[3] In conjunction with the figures given above, it would seem that Mallon has been put in his place and the record of the Fund proceeds untarnished.

But there is a more fundamental criticism to be made, one missed by Mallon and not so easily refuted by the board. It is a criticism which arises from the consideration of how the board decides to allocate its money. Speaking in the House of Commons in March 1988, Peter Viggers spelt out the procedure as follows:

> 'The International Fund for Ireland is administered by an independent board appointed by the United Kingdom and Irish governments ... the board has delegated to specialist agencies, *including some government departments*, responsibility for the administration of its various programmes ... '[4]

The significance of this admission cannot be underestimated. It would be nice to think that perhaps the tail could wag the dog, that the board of the International Fund could dictate procedures to one of the NIO's most powerful Departments. But, although Viggers assured MPs that these government Departments administer the Fund's money in line with 'criteria and operating arrangements specified by the board,' there is one over-riding criterion which the DED imposes, and the board is powerless to contradict, even if it wanted to. This is contained in Article

3 of the bilateral agreement between the UK and Southern Ireland which established the Fund.

> 'These disbursements shall be consistent with the economic and social policies and priorities of the respective governments.'[5]

In other words the criteria for allocation of funds are so broad and non-specific that Viggers might have revealed as much about government policy by saying that the Fund's money will go to groups the NIO want it to go to, and not to groups it does not want supported. There are no rational criteria of allocation spelt out, no notion of funding on the basis of merit. Instead it is in effect stated that funding will be discretionary.

The immediate implications of such a procedure for places like the Conway Mill, already mentioned, are clear, as Viggers pointed out:

> 'The United Kingdom government have advised the board of the International Fund for Ireland that provision of support to Conway Community Development Enterprise Ltd in respect of activities at the Conway Street Mill is not consistent with the government's economic and social policies and priorities.'

And, like a faithful lapdog, the board conveyed the message to the management at the Mill that it would not be funding any projects there because

> 'it would be inconsistent with the policies and priorities of the government of the United Kingdom to accede to your application'.[6]

The NIO is thus able to determine who does not get International Fund money. In addition, such money from the Fund which goes to West Belfast allows the NIO to solve the problem of being seen to be doing something about the unemployment problem of the area without actually having to put up much money itself. It thus has the best of both worlds, managing the allocation of funds and determining the criteria of that allocation without having to be out of pocket at all.

Recently the EEC has contributed to this face-saving exercise for the NIO by pumping £27 million into the Fund's coffers. Interestingly, the EEC would gladly have put in more money had the UK government not blocked them.[7] £27 million represented the limits of what the North could receive before money would be subtracted from rebates promised to the British government for other areas of the United Kingdom. In short, additional EEC money would have incurred a real redistribution of funds between Britain and the North. Once again it was clear that political priorities rather than EEC definitions of need determined British government economic decisions.

European Community Finances

Even more spectacular than the DED's domination of the International

Fund has been what can only be termed its hijack of EEC funds to the North. Between 1973 and 1986 Northern Ireland received the amounts shown in Table 8.2 from EEC funds.

Table 8.2: *EEC Funds in Northern Ireland 1973 to 1986.*[8]

European Agricultural Guidance and Guarantee Fund	£625.4m
European Regional Development Fund	£150.1m
European Social Fund	£273.6m
Special Measures for the UK	£294.6m
Urban Renewal	£52.4m
TOTAL	£1,396.1m

The extent of the hijack, as well as what it has meant specifically for West Belfast, can be seen if three of those categories are examined in detail.

It is also evident from the fact that an approach to the European Community Office in Belfast for accurate information on EEC aid to West Belfast was met with the suggestion to 'try the European Community section of the DED'. The European Community Office did not have carefully compiled data. On the contrary, their files on each of the Funds mentioned above contained press releases from Stormont, newspaper cuttings and documentation from Brussels. We were allowed access to these files, but, given the fact that the data we had to work with were presented in such a raw state, we cannot be sure that the information on which the rest of this section is based is comprehensive. Nor can we guarantee that the definition of West Belfast always coincides with that used throughout this report. However, in the absence of an alternative and more reliable source of information we have used this source to examine the extent of European Community funding to West Belfast.

a.) European Social Fund

Between 1982 and 1987 the European Social Fund provided £278,552,197 for the North. The vast bulk of this went directly to government Departments under the general title 'vocational training and guidance'. For instance:

Department of Economic Development	£196,566,145
Department of Education	£22,694,881
Department of Health and Social Services	£12,941,560

In addition, these government Departments were responsible for processing and allocating the funds received; all the money from the European Social Fund went through them, even if going to independent voluntary bodies such as those listed below. These Departments suggested which projects other than ones run by themselves should get what money, and later they became the managers of the money to those projects when the EEC delivered it to them. Some major amounts thus went to semi-government organisations; between 1982 and 1985, the Northern Ireland Electricity Service received £3,705,050, while Shorts got £3,398,538, and Harland and Wolff, £2,677,120.

After all this money was allocated, very little was left over for other projects, *eg*:

Enterprise Carrickfergus	£239,800
NIACRO	£131,153
Dismas House	£48,311
Derry Film and Video Association	£27,703
Craigavon Women's Development Project	£27,234

It could be argued that the benefits of this money accrue proportionately to West Belfast through training schemes, ACE employment, etc. or that residents of West Belfast participate in such projects even if they are located outside the area. But there are a number of counters to such an argument. Firstly, those individual projects outside of government departments which acquired large sums of money are all well-established firms (Harland and Wolff, Shorts). There are few such firms in West Belfast eligible for large amounts of money.

Secondly, it is well-known from FEA reports and investigations that Catholics, from West Belfast and elsewhere, are under-represented in such established firms, as well as in the government departments which were the largest recipients of funds.[9]

b.) European Regional Development Fund

European Regional Development Fund grants are divided into two sections, Industry grants and Infrastructure grants. Table 8.3 shows the allocations for 1985 and 1986.

Table 8.3: *EEC Regional Development Fund Allocations, 1985 and 1986.*

INDUSTRY	
West Belfast	£224,887
Belfast	£1,270,722
Northern Ireland	£10,428,819
INFRASTRUCTURE	
West Belfast	£803,890
Belfast	£3,079,390
Northern Ireland	£12,762,470
TOTAL	
West Belfast	£1,028,777
Belfast	£4,350,112
Northern Ireland	£23,191,289

To first appearances, West Belfast has done well; it accounts for 18% of Belfast's Industry allocation and 26% of Belfast's Infrastructure allocation, i.e. 24% of all allocations for Belfast from the European Regional Development Fund in these two years.

But, Belfast has not done too well relative to the North overall—12% of the Northern Ireland total for Industry, and 24% of the Northern Ireland total for Infrastructure. Belfast has received 19% of all Northern Ireland allocations in these two years.

So, West Belfast Industry allocations account for 2% of Northern Ireland Industry allocations and its Infrastructure allocations for 6% of Northern Ireland Infrastructure allocations, i.e West Belfast's total allocations from the European Regional Development Fund in these two years were 4% of all Northern Ireland allocations, this in an area with almost 10% of Northern Ireland's unemployment.

c.) Integrated Operations

It could be argued that the diversion of funds from Belfast is justified given that the so-called Integrated Operations package brought a vast amount of money to the city in the half decade before this. In fact, it appears that the extra funding to Belfast from the European Community, over and above what it would have given anyway, was only in the region of £56m. But everything that was done in Belfast with European Community funds in the first half of the 1980s came to be grouped under the heading of Integrated Operations, whether it was paid for by this extra money, European Social Fund money, European Regional Development Fund money, or indeed Northern Ireland Office money. All this money was allocated in three phases, or 'schedules', as shown in Table 8.4.

Table 8.4: *Spending Under Integrated Operations.*[10]

	Schedule 1	Schedule 2	Schedule 3	TOTAL
	£360,100,000	£170,100,000	£228,400,000	£758,600,000
of which West Belfast received:	£25,124,000 (7%)	£1,584,000 (1%)	£3,200,000 (1%)	£29,908,000 (4%)
and further:	of this, £16,791,000 (67%) went to house building.	of this, £1,000,000 (63%) went to road works in the North Howard Street/Northumberland Street area.	of this, £2,700,000 (69%) went on building a factory, small units and 'rejuvenation' of North Howard Street.	

Admittedly, some of the schemes which were not funded for one specific geographical area—such as Department of the Environment street lighting schemes, Department of Agriculture sewerage schemes—might have benefited West Belfast in proportion to other areas. But, even if this is so, why has the area with the highest rates of unemployment in Belfast received so little of the funding for the renewal of Belfast? It could be argued that the area did not need merely proportional treatment (which it clearly did not receive), but affirmative action in relation to such funding. Moreover, within the money which actually got to West Belfast, the vast amount was spent on things—housing, road works, etc.—which the Department of the Environment should have been doing for the area anyway, without such large injections of EEC funds.

The hijacking of EEC funds was done with the connivance of the EEC itself, in as far as it allowed the NIO to act in effect as its plenipotentiary. This is not to say that the EEC was happy with every aspect of the NIO's stewardship of its funds. In particular, the question of 'additionality' of funds has been a major source of friction between the NIO and the EEC (see Figure 8.1). What is clear is that the NIO has done remarkably well out of EEC financing, while West Belfast has not. Officially, EEC funding covers 50% of government costs involved in running ACE; in fact, such is the scale of EEC funding that most of what happens under ACE, YTP and other training schemes (see Chapter 9) is done at little or no cost to the NIO. What West Belfast gains is a miniscule amount of the total funding, dubious training schemes turning people out with few skills or skills that allow them little access to local jobs, or various manoeuvres to mask unemployment. EEC funding, as managed by the DED and other government departments, has done next to nothing to create real and meaningful jobs for West Belfast.

Figure 8.1

Arguments Over Additionality

In March 1981 the House of Lords Select Committee on the European Community accused the government of pocketing European Community money to pay for projects it was undertaking anyway rather than using it as extra to planned expenditure. In relation to the European Regional Fund, for example, the Select Committee stated that the money received had 'caused very little to happen that would not have happened anyway, and that the principle of additionality was largely disregarded in practice' (*Belfast Telegraph* 12/3/81).

In the same vein *Belfast Telegraph* European correspondent John Humphries accused the government of systematically raiding 'the Fund to help finance their public sector borrowing requirement ... the UK Treasury, acting within the government's tight financial guidelines, was effectively the sole arbiter of how our share of the Fund would be used ... the pathetically small £371m to be distributed among the entire Community this year stood little chance of being applied as was originally intended to inject additional resources into the less prosperous areas. The British share has already been skillfully diverted into existing expenditure programmes designed only to support the regions, but certainly not enhance them' (*Belfast Telegraph* 29/4/81).

By way of defence of the government against such criticisms, the Northern Ireland Economic Council justified the practice of non-additionality in terms surely reminiscent of the government's own sentiments.

> '... European community grants are counted as part of United Kingdom public expenditure in Northern Ireland and public expenditure remains unchanged ... However, European community receipts allow total public expenditure to be set at a higher level than would otherwise be the case.'[11]

Conclusion: Centralism and Control

It would appear that in relation to any moves to counter unemployment in the North, all roads lead to the DED. It funds the IDB and LEDU, which between them account for the bulk of job creation outside the private sector. Moreover, the DED is the recipient of vast sums of money from the EEC and increasing amounts of aid from the International Fund for Ireland. As a result of these handouts from abroad, the NIO is sitting very comfortably, with the EEC and the International Fund paying a major proportion of the cost of doing what the NIO should be doing anyway in terms of job creation. This criticism could be muted somewhat if real jobs were being created instead of the seemingly endless proliferation of ACE and 'training' schemes which often do not lead to real jobs. In addition, if it could be shown that the distribution of these funds was fair—that is, received by specific areas in proportion to their need—then recipients of the jobs created would surely be content to leave the government, the EEC and the International Fund to argue out the finer points of 'additionality' and continue drawing their wages.

But the major problem as regards the DED'S ubiquity in relation to job creation is that it is more than a mere neutral channel for funds. As has been shown above, its political priorities determine the allocation of these funds and consequently result in an unfair distribution.

In 1982 a group of economists, business people and trade unionists in the North stated the case against the DED and other NIO Departments, arguing that they had 'a concentration of economic decision making power ... greater than in any other Western European country'.[12] As a result, 'a proper informed dialogue on the economy of Northern Ireland between government officials and other parties does not take place. The current position is one where those in authority are willing to listen, but are not willing to expose their own thinking to critical scrutiny.' These critics were arguing from a self-protective professional standpoint; they were displeased that the NIO Departments were content to arrive at decisions without their expert professional assistance. But, if such a strong criticism can emerge from such conservative circles, an even stronger condemnation is possible if one is considering the DED's failure to revive the most economically beleagured areas in our society.

West Belfast has acquired a scandalously low level of assistance through all the sources of funding for job creation controlled by the DED. As our evidence has shown, West Belfast has historically fared badly compared to other areas such as the growth centres outside Belfast. Yet on the basis of need West Belfast requires a major programme of affirmative action in relation to job creation.

The mechanisms of neglect in recent years are different from what they used to be. In the days of the Unionist government it was easy to see Catholic West Belfast in particular as the victim of state discrimination. With Labour direct rule, there was a significant reversal of previous policy and West Belfast for a while was favoured with major job creation initiatives. But the combination of global recession and Tory direct rule meant the end of that partial revival. The current team of NIO ministers (unlike Jim Prior and others previously) are not Tory wets banished to the wilderness for their sins. They are dedicated followers of monetarist fashion. So, the kindest conclusion that one can draw is that the exercise of monetarism in relation to job creation automatically disadvantages already disadvantaged areas like West Belfast. Investment goes where success seems surest—to Ballymena and Newtownabbey rather than benighted West Belfast—*and there is nothing that free market proponents would want to do to counter that tendency*. The IDB and LEDU, for example, *react* to investment demands; they do not consider a proactive role in relation to areas like West Belfast. So, the logic of free market forces may be all the explanation required for the continuing unfair distribution of resources. Unlike in the days of Unionist rule, there may be nothing overtly sectarian in the fact that West Belfast continues to suffer.

But of course it is much more than this. The free market does not exist, especially not in a society where such economic decision making power ('greater than in any other Western European country') is concentrated in the hands of a few government Departments. These Departments are agents for translating Tory ideology into practice. As such, they are active determinants of the distribution of capital. This is shown most clearly in relation to the vetting of projects in such a way that the funding for Catholic West Belfast, whether government generated or acquired from bodies such as the EEC, is being channelled according to political criteria rather than on the basis of merit and strategic economic planning. As Chapter 9 underlines in relation specifically to the future of training schemes in West Belfast, the move is towards supporting Catholic church-backed groups rather than those which are independent of church control. More starkly, as Chapter 10 reveals, political criteria determine the removal of funding from any groups judged by the NIO to be IRA fronts.

In the last two decades at least West Belfast has not been a government priority in any sense other than 'security'. During that period the economic problems of the area were more or less ignored. Now that the area's economic problems have moved closer to the centre of the political stage the conclusion must be that 'security' rather than economic development as such is still a major determinant of government action. Not only is the money which has recently and belatedly been directed towards the area insufficient for economic recovery, but it is also being used for political ends, building up supposedly safe church-backed groups to the detriment of other groups involved in economic initiatives in the area.

Footnotes

1. *Belfast Telegraph* 10/12/87.
2. *Irish News* 15/6/88.
3. *Belfast Telegraph* 15/6/88. On the other hand the Board of the International Fund for Ireland in effect later admitted the substance of such criticisms. Having received a further $35 from the US Congress, it stated that some of this would be targeted on 'the most disadvantaged areas of Northern Ireland' (cited in *Irish News* 9/9/88). Although £3m was earmarked for 'community economic regeneration' and a further £3m for 'possible projects in those areas which might not satisfy all the criteria required by its existing programmes', the mechanisms of the change of direction were not spelt out in any detail.
4. Hansard 14/3/88; our emphasis.

5. In this vein, it is symbolic that the International Fund for Ireland board is not only appointed by the NIO, but operates out of a suite of four offices in Stormont.
6. Letter of Peter Viggers to Conway Development Enterprise Limited, 8/2/88.
7. See John Hume's complaint on this matter, *Belfast Telegraph*26/5/88.
8. Source: *Economic Implications for Northern Ireland and the Republic of Ireland of Recent Developments in the European Community*, Northern Ireland Economic Council/National Economic and Science Council, February 1988; table 4.7.
9. See for example, Fair Employment Agency, *A Final Report of the Fair Employment Agency for Northern Ireland into the Employment Practices of the Northern Ireland Electricity Service*, Belfast 1982; and *Engineering Investigation and Report*, Belfast, n.d.
10. See internal report, European Community Office, Belfast.
11. Northern Ireland Economic Council, *Additionality of European Community Funds: Submission to Assembly Finance and Personnel Committee*, Belfast: Northern Ireland Economic Council, Paper 2, February 1983, p. 4.
12. *Unemployment: Recommendations for Action within a Strategy for Economic Development*, Belfast, 1982.

9.

Special Employment Measures, Training and West Belfast

Introduction

In the North (as in Britain) there is a plethora of government employment and training schemes—preparing the young unemployed for acquiring jobs, retraining redundant adults, providing low paid work for the long-term unemployed, and so on. Together they include a substantial number of people who would otherwise be counted among the unemployed, as the figures for June 1988 reveal (Table 9.1).

Table 9.1: *Participants in Training and Special Measures.*[1]

Adults in training centres	750
Adults in Attachment Training (skills not available in training centres)	650
Management Training Schemes	100
Enterprise Allowance Scheme (to enable self-employed to establish selves)	2,100
Adults in Enterprise Ulster (construction projects, for environment/amenities	1,400
Action for Community Employment	8,550
Youth Training Programme:	
Guaranteed First Year Training	6,050
Second Year Training	1,300
TOTAL	20,900

According to the government, such a substantial number of people removed from the category of the unemployed is proof of its commitment to do all it can to solve the problem of unemployment, in particular, youth unemployment and long-term unemployment. As further evidence, the government would point to the fact that the number of schemes and the number of people involved in them have grown in line with the problem of unemployment itself. Critics are quick to retort that this growth represents a frantic attempt by government to mask the true levels of unemployment.[2] The critics argue firstly, that even after the removal of a large number of people from the unemployed register, the levels of long-term unemployment and youth unemployment are still unacceptably high. Secondly, these schemes do not of themselves make the participants any more likely to acquire jobs.

This second criticism is crucial in that it questions the relationship between training and employability. In this chapter we shall consider the two main schemes for the unemployed, the Youth Training Programme, geared towards unemployed school leavers, and Action for Community Employment, aimed at countering long-term unemployment. The conclusion is that the former programme falls short of matching training to employability by training young people for jobs which do not exist, or putting increasing emphasis on encouraging the unemployed to change their attitudes in order to make themselves more employable. Such an approach is no substitute for the twin strategy of making jobs available and training people in the skills needed for those jobs. In relation to ACE the fact that there is little or no training content involved in practice means that there is no discernible relation between participation in this scheme and subsequent employability.

The Youth Training Programme (YTP)

YTP is in fact a complex cluster of elements all supposedly geared to training young unemployed people and thus making them more employable.

We estimate that West Belfast contains slightly over 10% of all the unemployed 16 and 17 year olds in the North. YTP therefore ought to be of crucial importance to the area. Unfortunately, sufficient detail on the operations of YTP in West Belfast is not available. However, it is possible not only to chart what is involved in YTP, but also to give some indication of West Belfast's position in relation to the programme overall.

1. Guaranteed Year Training Provision

One year of training is guaranteed to (but not taken up by) all unemployed school leavers. The year is spent in one of the following locations:

a. Further Education College: 25 of the North's 26 Colleges participate. Courses last up to 45 weeks and provide either specific or general vocational preparation. Day release courses are also run for those in other schemes under YTP. A major element in 16 of the Colleges is Youthways, with strong emphasis on young people bettering themselves to be more acceptable to employers.

West Belfast has only recently acquired an extension of Rupert

Stanley College. Up until this point young people from the area have had to travel to Rupert Stanley College (in East Belfast) or the College of Business Studies or the College of Technology (in Central Belfast) to participate.

b. Community Workshops: there are 44 in the North. They provide training in specific skills, ranging from light engineering to horticulture. There is a clear sexual division of labour, with girls for the most part concentrated in stitching (often given a more grand title, such as 'Textile Crafts') and boys spread over a wide range of skills.

In West Belfast there are 12 YTP schemes currently providing full time places for 841 young people.[3] They include Scala Community Workshop with 95 places (not all of which are occupied at any one time), Lower Falls Training Workshop (125 places), Glenand Youth and Community Workshop (155 places), Colinbrook Community Workshop (90 places), Fallswater Training Centre (55 places) and Clowney Youth Training Workshop (120 places).

c. Government Training Centres: there are 12 in the North, 11 of which participate in YTP. They provide:

i. 6 months broad-based Basic Vocational Training, *eg* plastering, computers;
ii. 6 months Apprentice Training or Advanced Vocational Training, that is, for the most part preparation for semi-skilled work in the construction and engineering industries.

The closest Government Training Centre to West Belfast is at Boucher Road. It participates in all aspects of YTP and seems to provide as wide a range of training skills as any other Government Training Centre.

2. Second Year Training

A second year of training is available on YTP. It can be spent in one of the following locations.

a. Community Workshops: participants continue learning skills and other tasks begun in the first year at a more advanced level. But, as YTP managers themselves reluctantly admit, 'a major disappointment of many Workshops has been their lack of success in persuading 17 year olds to join the second year courses on offer'.[4]

b. Youth Community Projects: 18 in the North. Projects undertaken are specifically in the areas of environmental improvement, construction, community services and youth work.

c. Young Help: working with the elderly, handicapped, children, *etc.* Mainly confined to females on YTP.

d. Further Education Colleges.

3. Additional Elements in YTP

In addition, there are two schemes for already employed young people which come under YTP. They are:

a. Workscheme: for 17 year olds in employment. Employers are encouraged to release them for further education in Colleges or further training in Government Training Centres or Community Workshops.

   Between March 1987 and January 1988 1,811 young people from the Greater Belfast area were approved for participation in Workscheme.[5] The numbers specifically from West Belfast are not obtainable.

b. Skill Training Scheme: grants of up to £3,000 are made to employers to enable employees to gain proper apprentice training and certification.

YTP is the front runner in the government's claims to be doing something to increase the employability of the young unemployed. Consequently, the assertion is that the majority of YTP leavers get jobs. Peter Viggers backed this claim up with statistical evidence in a parliamentary answer in December 1987 (see Table 9.2).

Table 9.2: *Known Destinations of YTP Leavers, 1984/5 to 1986/7.*[6]

	Employment	Further Education	Unemployment
1984/5	55%	3%	42%
1985/6	57%	3%	40%
1986/7	54%	4%	41%

Even if the figures were reliable, they would be less than overwhelming proof of a central plank of Tory ideology, the claim that training leads to employability and therefore employment. Only slightly over half of the participants of YTP moved on to employment.

But the figures are open to question. The above percentages relate *only* to those YTP leavers whose destinations are known. Between September 1982 and March 1985, there were 23,218 YTP leavers; the destinations of only 18,960 of these were known.[7] 4,258 leavers—18.3% of all those who passed through the schemes in that period—were unclassified.

For some of the YTP elements, the lack of statistical information is highly significant given the large number of leavers who are unclassified (see Table 9.3).

Table 9.3: *Destinations of Leavers from Various YTP Schemes, 1984/5 to 1986/7.*[8]

	YTP SCHEME			
	Further Education	Community Workshop	Training Centres	Work Experience
Total leavers	3,962	8,144	4,574	3,255
Leavers whose destination is known	3,615	5,869	4,304	3,110
Leavers whose destination is unknown as percentage of total leavers	8.8	27.9	5.9	4.5

Including the unknowns in the figures, changes the picture radically, as Table 9.4 shows.

Table 9.4: *Destinations of all YTP Leavers, 1984/5 to 1986/7.*

	Number	Percentage of leavers whose destination is known	Percentage of all leavers
Employed	10,049	53	43.3
Unemployed	8,532	45	36.7
Further Education	379	2	1.6
SUBTOTAL	18,960	100	
Unknown	4,258		18.3
TOTAL	23,218		100.0

So it is clear that only a minority of those leaving the YTP schemes are *known* to have gained employment, a significantly different way of making the point from that of Peter Viggers.

What of the 18.3% unknowns? It cannot be presumed that they all acquired jobs. On the other hand, if only two thirds of them became unemployed on leaving YTP, then only a minority of those who had passed through YTP would have moved on to subsequent employment.

Equally crucial, and equally hidden, is the question of causation. What proof is there that the time the young person spent on YTP was the key element in their later obtaining a job? There is no direct evidence on this matter. In fact, when specifically asked in the House of Commons about that aspect of YTP where the connection would seem most likely, that is, young people gaining employment in firms where they had previously been placed in work experience, Peter Viggers stated:

> 'Separate records have not been kept of the number who find jobs with the employer who provided them with full-time training'.[9]

The YTP's own *Step in the Right Direction* is equally non-committal on this point.

> 'A considerable number of trainees undergoing work experience have subsequently been offered a permanent job by the employers with whom they were placed.'

If anything, what little evidence there is reveals that at least one element of such work experience schemes is that employers use them to *exclude* young people from later jobs with their firm on the basis of judgements about their reliability, commitment to hard work, docility, *etc.*[10]

The question which follows is, if the YTP is not about direct training for employment, what is it about? One conclusion is that it exists to instil conservative values in young people. Youth unemployment (like unemployment in general) has been redefined. No longer is it seen as a result of structural problems and hence an actual lack of jobs, but it is said to derive from characteristics of the unemployed themselves. The solution is thus presumed to rest in the efforts of the unemployed to 'brush up their image' in order to impress potential employers. But there are at least two problems with such a proposed solution.

Firstly, there is clear evidence from Britain that employers do not particularly want young unemployed people to become too specialised. It is not their lack of specialism that excludes them from many jobs, but their youth. Employers are happiest when hiring males who are older and who have the commitments of a wife, children and a mortgage.[11] Such people have a reason to want to hold on to a job rather than to be highly mobile. Trapped as they are socially, they are captive employees, and as such they can be trained on the job. Most importantly for such employers, training on the job allows the employer to instil the specific ethos of the firm rather than simply a dexterous skill. The relationship between training and employment is thus a reversal of what Tory wisdom would have it. Certainly, the absence of training is not in itself necessarily a hindrance to employment, all other things being equal. Indirect proof of this is provided in the West Belfast context by places like Strathearn Audio and De Lorean. In each case the absence of an initially untrained workforce did not prevent the firms in question producing viable products. West Belfast workers were eager and quick to learn the skills once those skills were connected to real jobs.

Secondly, 'brushing up one's image' in at least some elements of the YTP schemes does not involve learning any particular dexterity; rather, it involves quite simply lowering one's expectations and aspirations in order to match the employment climate—that is, making oneself more exploitable. Certainly, this was the barely coded message of the *Holland Report* (1977) which led to the establishment of the Youth Opportunities Programme, the precursor of YTP. It urged the government to 'instil greater motivation in the young unemployed and make them more attractive to potential employers.'

Consequently, the Youthways element of YTP is designed

> 'to try to improve young people's self-confidence, help them relate better to society in general and help them become more attractive to employers.'[12]

This approach comes across most clearly in the social and life skills classes in YTP, where trainees are supposed to be taught how to 'resist provocation, accept authority, take orders', and where the most widely used text book gives the following words of wisdom to the young unemployed: '... the boss ... has more problems than you ... the boss is probably doing a fairly good job or he wouldn't be where he is'.[13]

The lack of a strong proven link between training and employment, the emphasis on 'individual improvement' rather than real skills, the mindlessness of many of the placements on work experience, the regimentation in many YTP Community Workshops and the conviction that YTP is a substitution rather than a preparation for employment—all these are criticisms of the scheme which are much more than merely academic. The belief of many unemployed school leavers that such criticisms are valid has led them to ignore YTP altogether. Even the government in its glossiest and most glowing appraisals of the scheme has to acknowledge this. For example, although 5,000 full-time training places were created for 17 year olds in a second year training programme in Community Workshops,

> 'actual occupancy of these training places was disappointly low ... Despite strenuous efforts by Careers Officers and scheme organisers, it was apparent that many unemployed 17 year olds were not taking up the training places available.'[14]

In fact, at any one time many of the YTP elements are under-utilised. For example, Lower Falls Youth Training Workshop had only 86 trainees in February 1988 instead of the maximum 125 allowed.[15]

Another measure of disinterest is the downright refusal of some young unemployed people to participate in YTP even when given a definite place on the scheme. For the North as a whole 6,659 people refused YTP places between 1983/4 and 1986/7, as shown in Table 9.5.

Table 9.5: *Refusals on YTP Schemes, 1983/4 to 1986/7.*[16]

1983/4	2,348
1984/5	1,974
1985/6	1,080
1986/7	1,257
TOTAL	6,659

In addition, many young people who take up YTP places do not complete the programme. The most that the government wishes to reveal in relation to such people is that records of premature leavers are not recorded.

Given this clear tendency for the young unemployed to vote with their feet in relation to YTP, the government has been considering ways to force them to participate. The easiest method is to withdraw benefits from those otherwise eligible for them unless they take a YTP place. In this light, a recent warning from the President of Rupert Stanley College Students' Union in Belfast is timely.[17] Proposed DHSS changes, he claimed, will ensure that YTP will in effect become compulsory for all unemployed school leavers. Instead of being given quality training in skilled jobs, the young unemployed will be forced into a scheme which guarantees cheap labour for employers.

Critics in Britain, such as the TUC, have seen these moves as a fundamental attack on the post-war welfare principle. They argue that 'workfare' is about to replace 'welfare,' that is, forcing people to 'earn' their benefits rather than obtain them as of right. As we shall now see, a similar principle is on the cards in relation to the long-term unemployed.

Action for Community Employment

Action for Community Employment (ACE) is the equivalent of the Community Programme in Britain. Modelled on the British programme it is supposed to provide temporary jobs of up to one year in duration for long-term unemployed adults. The scheme began in 1981 with 430 participants.[18] It built up rapidly through the years to the current level of 6,200 employees, and has cost £135.15m to run between 1981 and the present.[19] In scale it now almost matches the YTP, and is presented by the government as the cutting edge of its fight against long-term unemployment, just as YTP is said to be in the vanguard of the fight against youth unemployment.

However, there is one major difference between YTP and ACE. The former may be in many ways inadequate training, but the latter in practice hardly functions as a training scheme at all. Although the rules allow for employees to be sent on relevant training courses provided under other auspices, most employers are not aware of such courses or are not eager to send employees on them. In addition, most ACE workers seem unaware of their right to participate in such courses and therefore do not make demands to do so on employers. Moreover, although criticisms can be made of the government's grandiose claims of the link between YTP and subsequent employment, there is by definition no such link in the case of ACE; ACE workers can only be employed for up to one year. Given these facts and the mundane nature of the work involved for many ACE workers, it is very difficult to present ACE in any other light than as a way to take the long-term unemployed off the unemployed register temporarily thus making the extent of long-term unemployment appear less obvious. Those who re-join the ranks of the unemployed after an ACE contract are regarded statistically as 'newly unemployed'.

These criticisms are especially relevant in relation to West Belfast. The area was involved in ACE projects from the beginning, and as the scheme built up, so did the stake of West Belfast in it. Of the 80 ACE projects in the North employing more than 10 ACE workers as of October 1986, 14 were in West Belfast.[20] Some of these eventually became very large operations; Grosvenor Environmental Society, for example, had 120 ACE workers by 1988, while Cathedral Community Enterprises, an amalgamation of various Catholic church schemes (St. Agnes', St. Luke's, St. Oliver Plunkett's) rose to 186 ACE workers.

The point is even more starkly emphasised by the following figures. In January 1988 there were 6,200 ACE workers in the North; 1,174—almost 19%—of those were working in West Belfast.[21]

Given the concentration of ACE employment in West Belfast, the problems commonly cited in relation to ACE are of central relevance to the area. They include the following.

As it grew, ACE steamrolled over existing and valuable schemes. Enterprise Ulster, for example, established in 1973, exists to provide work in relatively large construction projects in the area of environment and amenities. Already by the end of 1980, some months before ACE began, the management of Enterprise Ulster issued a press statement of unprecedented anger, complaining that they were in danger of being reduced to the position of 'filling in holes and cleaning out sheughs'.[22] ACE has increasingly replaced elements of Enterprise Ulster's work, but those of its employees involved in environmental or amenity work are not involved in projects of equal scale or skill as those undertaken by Enterprise Ulster.

Secondly, despite assurances to the trade union movement, it is clear that ACE became a means of job displacement. As public sector cuts took effect and jobs were lost, it was no coincidence that a number of public bodies—such as local councils, the social services boards—began to employ increasing numbers of ACE workers. Often these workers were employed to do work which should have been done by employees in proper full-time permanent employment.

Thirdly, for many ACE workers the experience of work is one of indecision, monotony and a sense of a lack of substance. The job lasts only one year, not enough time to build up something lasting and substantial from scratch. In addition, those managing the schemes may themselves often be people pulled off the dole into projects they had no hand in designing. Even if projects are begun with the best of intention, it can be the case that more effort is put into acquiring DED funding than actually planning the aims, objectives, methods and day-to-day tasks of the workers. This is often left to the ACE worker him/herself.

On the job - ACE-employer Cathedral Community Enterprises.

De Lorean - the dream (above) and the nightmare (below).

Fourthly, for the individual ACE worker the job is not particularly rewarding. It lasts only one year at maximum, the worker may be quite isolated, working in a situation where there are no tried and tested structures of support. The pay is basic, there are no career possibilities and no material incentives to make a roaring success of the project. The fact that many ACE workers are hard-working and totally dedicated to their job derives from their own personal commitment. Yet for such workers the experience can be even more frustrating, leading as it does to inevitable unemployment at the end of a year.

Fifth, the pay is low. ACE employers are allowed £98 (before tax) a week for each full-time employee. This does not mean that each employee acquires that total amount. Administrative and other needs of the organisation can eat into the amount left over for pay. In addition, government policy for the last two years has been to persuade ACE employers to take on two part-time employees instead of one full-timer. From the government's point of view this is a statistically and ideologically valuable approach, removing two people from the unemployment register where before they could only remove one. For the part-time workers, however, the financial reward for the job is negligible. The move was partially justified in terms of providing opportunities for women with children. But the cost of providing alternative child care for those children can soon take up all of (or more than) the pay from a part-time ACE job.

Sixth, whether full-time or part-time, ACE workers, as temporary employees, have not the same legal rights as employees on full-time contracts. In particular, they have no rights in relation to maternity pay, unfair dismissal or redundancy payments.

Seventh, the lack of training inherent in ACE employment has already been covered, but bears mentioning again. As a result of this lack, the ACE worker is no more likely to be employable at the end of the ACE year than s/he was before.

And finally, increasingly the DED has moved to centralise the whole ACE scheme under a number of big sponsors. In relation to West Belfast this in effect means the Catholic church has become the main and largest ACE employer in the area. The trend is revealed by government statistics. In November 1986, when there were approximately 700 ACE sponsors and 6,000 ACE jobs in the North, West Belfast had 55 ACE projects.[23] By January 1988 there were only 37 ACE projects in West Belfast,[24] even though the the number of ACE workers employed in West Belfast has expanded since 1986.[25] This coincided with the amalgamation of parish-based Catholic church ACE projects under the umbrella of Cathedral Community Entreprises and the increasingly closer links between Cathedral Community Enterprises and the NIO. The result of this centralisation overall has been not only that smaller ACE sponsors have found it increasingly difficult to obtain government assistance, but that even large sponsors, such as Grosvenor

Environmental Society, which are not under the church umbrella have found themselves facing contraction and possible demise.

The Future of Training and Special Measures

In September 1988 30 separate training schemes in Britain, including the Community Programme, their equivalent of ACE, are to be amalgamated under the Adult Training Programme. This change will not affect the North of Ireland in the first instance, but plans are afoot to introduce eventually 'corresponding proposals for Northern Ireland which take account of the local circumstances.'[26] Precisely what that coded message means we shall attempt to guess shortly. But whatever emerges, it is unlikely to be radically different from the imminent British programme. Given that, the criticisms of the British Adult Training Programme are likely to be relevant to the North also.

The Adult Training Programme is geared towards providing training for unemployed people, in particular the young and long-term unemployed. Instead of a wage, it will give participants £10 a week on top of their usual benefit. If travelling to training costs more than £5 a week, then they will get travel expenses; or, to put it another way, they could spend up to half their 'dole top-up' on travel without reimbursement. Single parents participating in the scheme will be eligible for up to £50 a week to provide for child care arrangements.

The TUC in Britain initially refused to back the proposed scheme. They had three main objections.

1. While the changes may benefit single parents and unemployed people with children, the young unemployed are likely to be worse off than under current arrangements.
2. No extra funding was to be provided to run the scheme, although there would be more people participating (600,000 a year) than in all the current schemes which are to be replaced.
3. There were strong hints in government statements about the programme that a 'workfare' principle would apply, namely, that claimants would be required to participate in the scheme under pain of losing their benefits (see Figure 9.1).

Figure 9.1

'Workfare' replaces 'Welfare'

It is apparent that the government is moving in the direction of 'workfare'. Already the London boroughs of Camden, Kensington and Chelsea, Brent and Westminster are operating on the basis that 'those long term unemployed people who refuse to accept jobs after visiting job clubs will have benefit withheld from them'[27] These boroughs have been carefully chosen as ones where the pool of jobs available is said to be relatively large. But once the ideological armour has been pierced on this point, it would appear to be only a matter of time until other areas, with fewer jobs available, will operate such a principle in order to force the unemployed off the registers and into 'work', no matter how mindless, dangerous or poorly paid.

In response to the likelihood of the TUC rejecting the proposals out of hand, the government made some concessions. It set aside an extra £45m to fund the Programme. In addition, it announced that bonuses would be available for participants in the programme, £50 after 6 months training successfully completed, and up to £250 on the successful completion of 12 months training. Consequently, in May 1988, the TUC voted by 19 to 14 to give the Adult Training Programme 'conditional support'.[28]

However, there are a number of major limitations in the scheme.

1. If the unemployed person quits the scheme before the end, s/he loses all right to unemployment benefit for 6 months.
2. The government has not spelt out the *training* content of the Adult *Training* Programme. There is thus no reason to feel reassured that it will in fact be any more substantial than the current provision of training under the Community Programme.
3. Department of Employment funding will only be given to training projects of 1,000 places or more. This will effectively wipe out the current involvement of the voluntary sector and local councils in the Community Programme. Few, if any, of these organisations will be able to provide such large-scale training projects. In effect, the Department of Employment will have a virtual monopoly over the provision of training. This fact has led the European Community to threaten to withdraw Social Fund money for training (currently £150m annually, 50% of the total cost) on the grounds that there will no longer be an independent control of training in Britain.[29]

It is only a matter of time before the North gets its own fully-fledged version of the Adult Training Programme. When it does, it is likely that it will contain a number of the same elements (and therefore be open to many of the same criticisms) as its precursor in Britain. Thus, it is likely that more people will be processed through the Programme than currently through YTP and ACE. Such people will receive a 'top up' to their dole benefit, and many will be worse off than they would have been in an ACE job. Moreover, there is likely to be as much initial imprecision in relation to the actual training content of the Programme as there is with the British scheme.

However, there will be one major difference between the British and Northern Ireland models, a difference which would account for Peter Viggers' cryptic comment, quoted earlier, that 'corresponding proposals for Northern Ireland' will 'take account of the local circumstances'. In Britain the current Community Programme (their equivalent of ACE) has led to a proliferation of schemes sponsored by the voluntary sector and local councils. A clear political purpose in replacing the Community Programme with the Adult Training Programme is to curtail the power of local councils, especially in areas such as Scotland where they are firmly in Labour's hands. In the process the voluntary sector's involvement in the Community Programme will be virtually obliterated, and the Youth Training Scheme will be run mainly by agencies specifically set up for the purpose.

The Tory government has no need to use the Adult Training Programme to identical political ends in the North. Local councils have used the ACE scheme, but they are not the target of government plans for curtailment, given that they are not Labour controlled and that they were already severely curtailed in the reorganisation of the early 1970s. Instead, the demise of ACE in the North has other political purposes. The voluntary sector has been heavily involved in sponsorship of ACE schemes in the North. But increasingly the smaller and more grass-roots groups in the voluntary sector have found it difficult to continue receiving or to obtain financial backing from the DED. The move has been towards the concentration of the management of ACE projects under a few 'super-sponsors' such as Bryson House in Belfast and the churches. In short, centralisation of training means that the NIO can cement alliances with the most conservative elements in the society, thus ensuring maximum social control. Furthermore, in the light of the contents of the following chapter, such elements cannot be accused of being channels whereby public funds find their way into the pockets of 'terrorists'.

In the West Belfast context it is quite clear that the preferred 'super-sponsor' is the Catholic church.[30] There are currently only a few major ACE schemes in Catholic West Belfast which are not under church control, and, if reports are correct, even those are finding continuing survival increasingly problematic. West Belfast's version of the Adult Training Programme will thus find most of the places under the more or less overt control of the Catholic church. The groundwork for the first of these is already under way with the announcement by Tom King (at the same time as reporting that £10m was to be made available for special initiatives in North and West Belfast) of 'a major package of support ... for the West Belfast Enterprise Board to help it establish a centre for enterprise development in the former American Monitor premises' on Kennedy Way.[31] A major element of the operations of this enterprise centre will be the provision of a 500-place training unit.

These developments are being presented, by the Catholic church hierarchy and the NIO alike, as important *community* initiatives in West Belfast. For example, after a meeting with members of the West Belfast Enterprise Board including Bishop Cathal Daly, Tom King reiterated his belief that 'if real and lasting progress is to be made, the local community has to be deeply and positively involved'.[32] But clearly the NIO is seeking a situation where there are definite levels of authority: the community groups are under church management and the church is highly susceptible to government influence because government Departments are the channel of all outside money (government, EEC and International Fund) which reaches West Belfast.

In a very real sense this process is not new, but merely a refinement and elaboration of government political maneoeuvres in relation to West Belfast which have been in operation for at least the last decade and a half. This is most starkly revealed in the case of those local initiatives which have been blocked by government action on the grounds of being IRA fronts. It is to the experience of those groups in West Belfast which we will now turn.

Footnotes

1. DED Press Release, 14/7/88. In addition to those who would otherwise be classified as unemployed if they were not on the schemes listed, there are other young people in the Youth Training Programme under two separate headings:

Training on Employers' Premises	4,239*
New Workers' Scheme (paying employers to provide jobs for young people 'at realistic wage rates')	969*
YTP Workscheme (day release for young employees)	7,400

*Places approved as of January 1988.

It is reasonable to conclude that these two schemes play a part in persuading employers to hold on to employees who might otherwise be unemployed.

2. See Hill, M., 'Government Responses to Unemployment', in M. Loney, D. Boswell and J. Clarke (eds), *Social Policy and Social Welfare*, Milton Keynes, Open University Press, 1983, pp. 241-254.
3. Letter from Peter Viggers, 7/1/88.
4. *A Step in the Right Direction: Youth Training Programme Review and Plan*, 1984, p. 14.

5. Letter from Peter Viggers, 7/1/88.
6. Hansard WA 17/12/87, col. 678.
7. Figures calculated from *A Step in the Right Direction.*
8. *Ibid.*
9. Hansard WA 17/12/87, col. 678.
10. See 'Youth Unemployment: Sweeping them under the Carpet', *Belfast Bulletin* 8, pp. 57-61.
11. See Pahl, R. and Wilson, P., *Industry and Training on the Isle of Sheppey in the 1980s*, Work Strategies Unit, University of Kent, 1986.
12 *A Step in the Right Direction*, p. 5.
13. Quoted in McCullagh, M. 'Youth Unemployment and the Ideology of Control', in C. Curtin, M. Kelly, and L. O'Dowd (eds), *Culture and Ideology in Ireland*, Galway: Galway University Press, 1984, p. 131.
14. *A Step in the Right Direction*, p. 14.
15. Personal correspondence from secretary of Lower Falls Youth Training Society, 11/2/88.
16. Hansard WA 12/11/87, col. 312.
17. *Irish News* 10/6/88.
18. Hansard WA 1/5/87, col. 253.
19. Hansard WA 15/7/87, col. 490 and 29/5/88, col. 301.
20. Hansard WA 15/7/87, cols. 492-3.
21. Letter from Peter Viggers, 7/1/88.
22. Enterprise Ulster Press release, 19/11/80.
23. Hansard WA 21/11/86, col. 386.
24. Letter from Peter Viggers, 7/1/88.
25. The latest expansion was when Tom King announced that the long-awaited government economic initiative for West Belfast would involve, among other elements, the creation of a further 500 ACE places in North and West Belfast. See *Irish News* 20/7/88.
26. Hansard WA 29/4/88, col. 302.
27. *The Guardian* 22/2/88.
28. *The Guardian* 26/5/88.
29 *The Guardian* 8/4/88.
30. For a detailed critique of the Catholic church's involvement in training and economic development in West Belfast, see Wilson, D. and Kearney, O., *West Belfast—The Way Forward?*, 1988.
31. *Irish News* 20/7/88. The International Fund for Ireland officially announced its decision to allocate £½m to the training unit to be based in the former American Monitor factory one month later. See *Irish News* 19/8/88.
32. Northern Ireland Information Service Press Release, 20/6/88.

10.

Vetting of Community Initiatives

Introduction

On June 27, 1985 Douglas Hurd, ex-Secretary of State for Northern Ireland and now Home Secretary, replied in parliament to a question raised by John Taylor, MP for Solihull.

> 'It is the government's policy to encourage voluntary and community based activity which has the genuine aim of improving social, environmental or economic conditions in areas of need, and various grant-aid schemes exist for such purposes. However, I am satisfied, from information available to me, that there are cases in which *some community groups or persons prominent in the direction or management of some community groups, have sufficiently close links with paramilitary organizations to give rise to a grave risk that to give support to those groups would have the effect of improving the standing and furthering the aims of a paramilitary organisation*, whether directly or indirectly. I do not consider that any such government funds would be in the public interest, and in any particular case in which I am satisfied that these conditions prevail no grant will be made.'

In the year following this statement, funding for ACE workers was removed from the MacAirt Naiscoil (an Irish-language nursery) in Short Strand, Belfast, Dove House in Derry, and Twinbrook Tenants' and Community Association in Belfast. Most significantly of all the withdrawal of ACE funding proved one more attempt by government to nail down the coffin lid on a job creation enterprise situated in the heart of West Belfast, the Conway Mill. We shall look at the history of government attacks on the Conway Mill soon. But it is necessary first to recall that this was not the first example of community initiatives, especially in relation to job provision, being thwarted by government. For the first major example, we have to go back to the case of the Whiterock Industrial Estate.

Whiterock Industrial Estate

On January 11, 1974, John Hume, then Stormont Minister of Commerce, announced that approximately £1m was to be spent on two new industrial estates in West Belfast. These were at Kennedy Way—where a 20 acre plot was to be developed by Strathearn Audio, a 100% government-owned endeavour—and Whiterock. The latter was being developed by a community organisation, Whiterock Co-operative Industrial Estates Ltd., in partnership with the Department of Commerce. The announcement was hailed as a remedy to the unemployment situation in West Belfast at that time.

The idea for the creation of an industrial estate at Whiterock had come from local Ballymurphy community activists. For a long time the Ballymurphy Tenants' Association had been convinced that the unemployment problem in the area had to be tackled. In 1968 the local school, St. Thomas', conducted a survey into unemployment in the area and discovered that 47% of heads of households were unemployed; this was at a time when there was a high level of employment both nationally and internationally.

Local people decided on a strategy of self-help. But, as Frank Cahill, founder member of Whiterock Co-operative Industrial Estates and a member of Ballymurphy Tenants' Association, explains, they were initially unsure of the strategy to adopt.

> 'We thought first of all small co-operatives might be the answer and having attempted some of these small units for employing ten or maybe twelve people we soon discovered that this was an utterly impossible way to make a dent in the massive problem. Then we thought about the possibility of acquiring a site to build factories to encourage the industrialists to come into the area and set up.'

The idea for the Whiterock Industrial Estate was born. Negotiations were immediately begun to acquire a nearby 13 acre plot of land for an industrial site. But the group did not have the £60,000 needed to purchase the land. This problem was solved by borrowing £1,000 to retain an option on the land. Then the group discovered that the land was in fact outside the Matthew stopline and hence no building work was permitted. Government Departments were approached and after some discussion agreed that the stopline could be bent so that plans could go ahead for the creation of an industrial estate.

Planning permission was acquired and the group had plans drawn up for forty units to be leased to industrialists or local businesses. In addition, the group felt that there was a great need for a local training centre. As Frank Cahill explains, young people from the area

> 'had to go to a Training Centre in Castlereagh Road or they had to go down to Whiteabbey. These were very dangerous areas at the time ... in fact there was a bus hijacked coming home from Castlereagh Training Centre and the young people were set upon, with the result that they couldn't go back to Castlereagh because of intimidation. Now that meant there was no training for the people of West Belfast at all. At that stage the local management

Roads to nowhere - Turf Lodge.

Fort Pegasus - replacement for Whiterock Industrial Estate.

Daily life on the Falls - harassing the black taxis (above) and an afternoon drinking session (below).

group decided to approach the Department of Manpower Services. The DMS agreed after consultation that they would set up a Training Centre in the Whiterock Industrial Estate.'

With the establishment of the Training Centre 119 young people, mostly from the local area, were receiving training annually. For the first time West Belfast had the experience of local training. The training units were set up in temporary wooden buildings and a further 30-place centre for retraining adults was added to the complex. This represented the only light engineering training in West Belfast. The Department of Commerce also provided security for the site.

After five years an atmosphere of uncertainty began to pervade the industrial site. The DMS had commenced work on the building of a Government Training Centre in Boucher Road in 1973 and by 1975 it was ready to open. Frank Cahill believes now with the benefit of hindsight that the DMS had decided to pull their resources out of the Whiterock Estate but did not do this in a straightforward, business-like manner for political and security reasons.

> 'Strange things began to happen, odd things we could never find an answer to. First of all Commerce said there would be no more money available for security people, so that the security was taken away ... Then during the course of time the British army, who had been billetted all around the area, needed access to that land, so they cut the fences all around the site so they had easy access in and out of it. That made the place very vulnerable. Then, strangest of all the things happening was that one of the buildings was set on fire in the early hours of the morning. A week later another building was burnt. And then another week, another building was burnt and then finally they were vandalised. But we don't know who the vandals were. There's never been an explanation for that.'

The Department of Manpower Services moved training to the Boucher Road centre, leaving two factories operating at the Whiterock Industrial Estate. One had been built by the local group at a cost of £60,000 and the other by the Department of Commerce. The units that remained were progresing satisfactorily.

However, in October 1979, workers reporting for work as usual on a Monday morning were halted by the British army. Frank Cahill takes up the story.

> 'They were put up against a wall. They were photographed. Their names were taken. Their addresses were taken. The owners of the factories were told that they would have two weeks to remove their equipment from the site. They would get a pass onto the site for the two weeks and after that they wouldn't be allowed in. There were protests about this, but there was nothing anyone could do about it. The ground was taken over by the British army as a base.'

The people who worked on the industrial site were told that they could have alternative premises at Kennedy Way, but this information was gleaned only after a period of negotiation with the Department of Commerce and at great financial inconvenience to the businesses concerned. For example, a candle-making firm had to attempt to keep in touch with customers, move their equipment and fulfill orders at the same time. They found it impossible to do so and as a result lost quite a number of customers. They did not get any compensation for these losses.

The initiative of the local Ballymurphy people in setting up an industrial estate and Training Centre was therefore trampled over for political and military considerations. Politically it was easy for government to dismiss any local protests over the action as Republican propaganda. Morover, the insinuation that some of those locals most involved in setting up the initiative had connections with Republicans was deemed to be further justification for not shedding too many tears over the demise of the project. Today one of the largest British military installations in Nationalist Belfast, Fort Pegasus, stands on the ground originally acquired by local people to help their unemployment problem through their own efforts.

West Belfast Taxi Association

A longer running story along the same lines, but with a happier ending, is that of the black taxis on the Falls Road.

A survey was carried out by the Department of Transport Studies of the University of Ulster on all shared taxi routes in Belfast on 20th March, 1986 and the results were presented at the 17th Public Transport Symposium—'Innovation in Public Transport'—at the University of Newcastle-upon-Tyne in April 1986. The survey indicated that the approximate yearly passenger count for the black taxis in the Falls area was 8,512,992. If other areas including the Shankill and Shore Road are included, the total stood at 12,207,312. Shared taxis are therefore the second largest public transport operator in the Belfast Urban Area, next only to Ulsterbus/Citybus.

The West Belfast Taxi Association, the first and largest of the black taxi operations in Belfast, currently oversees the operation of 275 taxi-drivers who provide a service from Castle Street to the suburbs of West Belfast. The actual structure of the Association is similar to that of a workers' co-operative with prospective drivers applying to the Association for membership, but the taxis are owner-operated and the drivers are in fact self-employed.

The Association is controlled by an elected committee, which has twelve members, but is managed by a Chairman who is a salaried staff member. The Association has an office with a staff of five. The taxis are purchased via the Association's contacts with the London taxi trade.

Maintenance and preparation for statutory vehicle examinations is conducted by the Association's garage staff and the Association has the Irish franchise for taxi spares from London Taxi International Ltd. Insurance is obtained, on an individual basis, via the Association.

The West Belfast Taxi Association today is therefore responsible for having an estimated 300 people in employment. This success was achieved by local people in spite of attempts by the authorities and some political parties to have the Association crushed.

The shared taxi operation in West Belfast evolved in the early 1970s. As bus services were withdrawn from some areas for long periods during civil unrest, some residents of the area used their own cars to take neighbours to work or school. Initially large numbers of people crowded into private cars which were very often not road-worthy, not properly licensed nor insured to carry passengers. The black taxis were introduced onto the Falls Road at this time by cab-drivers from the City Hall and Garfield Street. Gradually private cars were phased out and black taxis introduced.

Another element in the origin of the taxi service was the need for ex-internees to find employment. The fact that many of the drivers were ex-internees became one element in the government's opposition to the project.

It became apparent to the taxi drivers that some form of organisation was needed and, after a series of meetings, the Falls Taxi Association was formed. The initial work of the FTA was to regularise and co-ordinate the taxi service. Definite decisions had to be made in relation to routes, fares and the establishment of specific taxi ranks in the Castle Street area. The drivers had to ensure that the vehicles were road-worthy and fully insured. The taxis also required proper maintenance; hence a number of ancillary jobs sprang up. For example, the FTA started up the Westside Garage and body repair shop. In addition to this there were many other small backstreet garages.

The immediate response of the British government was to move against the FTA. One supposed justification for this was that many of the drivers were ex-internees. This was taken as proof that the taxis were being used as a lucrative source of funds for Republican 'terrorists'. A further consideration was financial. The Citybus Company, which had previously held a monopoly on public transport, was losing revenues to the black taxis. So, far from assisting an employment iniative in an area of such high unemployment, the British government did its best to eliminate the black taxi service.

Action against the FTA took a variety of forms. Firstly, there was a great deal of harassment of taxi drivers and their passengers by the British Army. But potentially more devastating in the long run was the fact that the taxi drivers found it difficult to get insurance. Due to pressure from the British government, the insurance companies classed them as high-risk and the insurance became very expensive. Since the taxis could not operate legally without insurance, they faced the prospect of being put out of business. The FTA discovered that they could provide their own insurance by depositing £15,000 under the Northern Ireland Road Traffic Act, section 15. Citybus and Ulsterbus were insured in this manner. The DOE then claimed that the deposit was not adequate coverage and proceeded to take legal action against the FTA. At this point an insurance firm named Curran/Conway offered alternative insurance through Crow Motor Policies. The latter lost a lot of government contracts temporarily as a result; previously they had insured the Civil Service and the Northern Ireland Fire Service and these contracts were not renewed.

During the 1970s, because of insurance difficulties, the taxis were technically owned by Westside Garage to ensure blanket coverage. However, again this was used against the taxi drivers. Taxi drivers were constantly having their taxis checked by the RUC and, if a defect was found, not only was the taxi driver fined but Westside Garage as well. In this respect a lot of money was lost due to payments of fines. Finally the FTA challenged this procedure through the courts and won the case.

Perhaps the best outline of the authorities' attitude to the black taxis is contained in a major DOE publication on transport strategy published in 1978.

> 'The Inspector recommended that black taxis' competition with the bus services should be eliminated by the enforcement of the present laws or by the acquisition of fresh powers, therefore creating a virtual monopoly. The Department recognises the difficulties which are created for the public transport system by the black taxi operations and agrees that the existing system is unsatisfactory. Court cases are currently pending in regard to the insurance and licensing of a number of black taxis and the RUC are devoting more effort to the enforcement of the law as it applies to them. Consideration is to be given to the need for further powers.'[1]

There was no attempt to commend the taxi drivers for generating employment for themselves and others, but rather to place the taxi drivers outside the law.

By 1980, such were the debts facing the FTA due to court costs and fines, that it went out of business and the West Belfast Taxi Association was formed. A reappraisal of the taxi business was undertaken by the new manager, Jim Neeson, who reorganised the financial and other management aspects of the Association. Debts were repaid, new offices were acquired at the Conway Mill and a new garage developed, also at the Mill. In addition to this, the West Belfast taxis managed to get the franchise on taxi replacement parts and opened up a spare parts shop at their office premises.

The Association also moved on to further job creation by starting an additional taxi route to Ardoyne in North Belfast and introducing a black taxi service to Derry. There are 25 drivers on the former route, and 45 driving for Derry Black Taxis. In spite of the fact that West Belfast Taxis have been responsible for job creation in Derry and Belfast, they have never received any financial assistance from the government. Some of the new taxi drivers take the advice of West Belfast taxis and apply for the £40 a week available under the Enterprise Allowance Scheme for people starting up a new business. However the Association itself has never received a single penny in the form of grants.

The government's attitude to the Falls Road black taxis is in direct variance with their plans for shared taxis in Britain. In Britain, shared taxi services have been made possible by the 1985 Transport Act and have been vigorously promoted by Westminster as part of a policy of deregulating the bus industry in order to increase competition. Mr. David Mitchell, British Minister for Transport, summed up the government's views when he stated on October 18, 1985:

> 'For too long the taxi trade has been shackled by legal restraints that have relegated you to a small corner of the transport world. This Bill breaks down these barriers and allows you to come into the market and provide a better and more efficient public transport system for us all. You have the vehicles, you have the local knowledge, you have the skills and you have a head start. This Bill represents a revolution for the taxi trade.'

The shared taxi operation in Belfast is exactly the type of public transport operation that Westminster is determined will succeed, yet the government through its agencies in Belfast has constantly sought and continues to attempt to stifle the progress of the black taxis.

Conway Mill

The case of the Conway Mill, therefore, fits into a pattern of state attempts over the last decade to stifle certain forms of community initiative in relation to economic development. The difference is that what was conveyed by innuendo in relation to the Whiterock Industrial Estate and the Falls Taxi Association was finally stated openly in relation to the Conway Mill—namely, that the government's attempts to thwart such initiatives were justified by unproven assertions of links between these projects and the IRA.

The Conway Mill is one of the old linen mills for which Belfast was once famous. Vacant since 1974, it was purchased in 1979 by the Pound Loney Social Club. Since the Club required only approximately one third of the Mill site, it gave over the rest to a company representing the local community, with the brief that the site should be developed for jobs, education, culture and local community general use. That company was Conway Street Community Development Projects Ltd.

and its Directors were Fr. Desmond Wilson, former curate of St. John's and educationalist, Frank Cahill, and Colm Bradley, law graduate and community worker employed by Belfast City Council. Wilson and Cahill had both been involved previously with the Whiterock Industrial Estate.

Writing to one charitable concern in May 1985, Colm Bradley explained the objectives of the Committee:

> 'The Conway Street Development Project is an integrated industrial, social and cultural project based in a disused mill just off the Falls Road in Belfast. The site is managed by a Committee of people with experience in job-creation, local development and community service. The Committee is a non-profit making body which hopes to develop the site as an industrial complex providing much needed jobs in this hard pressed area and giving encouragement to people with new commercial and industrial ideas. The site is within the Enterprise Zone which provides a unique opportunity for co-operation between a voluntary body like ourselves, the statutory authorities and the business world ... While the prime objective of the project is to provide and encourage job creation, we would envisage later developments, including projects in the fields of youth work, community action and community education, enjoying the facilities available on the site and benefiting from them. However, the prime need of the Falls Road is economic development and the job creation that comes with it ...'

At the same time Springhill Community House, already established as a community education project in West Belfast, was offered the second floor of the Mill rent-free as a community education centre. They gladly accepted the offer as it meant not only more space to accommodate their growing numbers of students, but a site on the main road which was accessible to more people. By the end of 1982 some progress was visible. The debris was removed, the first of four sections of heating was installed and a canteen, three classrooms, a television room, a theatre and a creche were built. The creche was an especially important addition to the facilities as it permitted women with small children to make use of the Centre.

The Trustees intended to divide the 90,000 square feet available in the Conway Mill into small business units which would have accommodated an estimated 50-90 operators. The units were to be made available at an economic rent and business management courses were to be made available as well. The New University of Ulster asssisted in running a number of pilot business management courses to find out exactly what courses would be best suited to potential Mill businesses. In addition, it was hoped to provide secretarial and book-keeping services for those starting up in business in the Mill.

The Conway Mill - with Social Security Office in foreground.

Inside Conway Mill - Frank Cahill & Des Wilson on the right.

Inside Conway Mill - The Creche which was closed after political vetting.

From the very beginning the Committee entered into discussions with government agencies such as LEDU, Enterprise Ulster and the Department of Economic Development with a view to having the Mill developed as an industrial base and a youth training centre. Initially the reponse from government agencies was favourable. As it was situated in the Enterprise Zone, the Conway Mill was entitled to be free of rates, planning permission and so on. During the course of 1983 and 1984, lengthy negotiations were conducted with the Belfast Enterprise Zone about placing a Youth Training Centre in the Mill. Officials from the Enterprise Zone went as far as to submit display designs for the outside of the Mill to indicate that it was part of the Zone. In August 1984, Colm Bradley received an invitation to submit information about the range of activities carried out at Conway Mill for the Enterprise Zone's promotional bulletin.

In May of the same year, negotiations had begun with Enterprise Zone officials to work out 'ways and means of finding funding for your project, particularly using Urban Development Grants'.[2]

At the same time the Department of Economic Development had permitted the Project to take on a couple of ACE workers. There were additional ACE workers attached to the education floor.

The Mill was on course to provide an estimated 250 jobs and a Training Centre—all this in a complex also housing an education floor and a cultural centre. An independent assessment carried out by LEDU concluded that the Mill was commercially viable and the way was prepared for the introduction of financial assistance which could lead to the development of the Mill. The Mill Trustees suggested a government investment of £40,000 towards the first phase of development and they hoped to raise a similar sum themselves. For such a large development, this was a modest request from the public purse—a mere £160 per job.

The Trustees of the Mill had meanwhile succeeded in leasing some of the Mill space to small businesses. Rents from the businesses permitted the Trustees to pay bills and undertake some small improvements to the building.

On the education floor exciting progress was being made. The Rupert Stanley College recognised the Conway Education Centre as an out-centre and paid the salaries of the part-time tutors on the instructions of the Belfast Education and Library Board. The Centre continued to operate as an integral part of the education project which originated in Springhill House, and received backing not only from the Rowntree Trust but from the Northern Ireland Voluntary Trust as well. The numbers of students taking 'O' and 'A' levels increased, with many students progressing to universities. Apart from the classes, the Education Project involved itself in a diversity of activities. The work of the project was featured in educational publications and also in programmes made by such bodies as the Open University. Visiting speakers and lecturers included many leading Irish writers whose visits were arranged in co-operation with the Arts Council and the Workers' Educational Association.

Just when real progress was being made at the Conway Mill, the government moved in to block further development. The first indication came with the withdrawal of ACE funding to the two creche workers at the Education Centre in 1985 on the grounds that they were 'a security risk', in line with government policy as outlined by Douglas Hurd on 27th June, 1985. The ACE workers were given no means of appealing the decision. The insinuations made in Hurd's speech to the Commons were purposely vague so that the ACE workers involved had no definitive grounds for a libel action. Eventually the other ACE workers in the Mill suffered the same fate, on the grounds that 'there were sufficient funds within the Project to fund workers ...'

The DED simply refused to continue funding more workers if they were to be working at Conway Mill. Other government agencies followed suit. For example, Frank Cahill recalled that when the Trustees 'approached LEDU with a view to setting up business units at Conway ... they were turned down without a full explanation. The LEDU consultant just said "people in high authority" had said "no".'

Figure 10.1

Crèches and Machine Guns

LEDU's attention to the unproven connections between the Conway Mill and the IRA are in stark contrast to its failure to notice more sinister developments under its very nose. Thus, police uncovered an arms factory in Ballynahinch, County Down, where a light engineering works, supposedly manufacturing bench saws, was also turning out machine guns for loyalist use. The firm had once been in reception of LEDU grants on the grounds that it was, in the words of LEDU's marketing director Dennis Babes, 'deemed to be financially viable and produced a good product' (cited in *Irish News* 9/9/88). In other words business criteria alone were the sole basis on which the decision had been made to fund the Ballynahinch firm. The Conway Mill, on the other hand, had to face the additional hurdle of spurious political vetting, thus ensuring it could not obtain funds to operate nothing more sinister than a crèche.

In the months that followed the NIO blocked off all funds to the Conway Mill and were supported in this action by SDLP councillor Brian Feeney. Speaking on RTE Radio 1 on 5th February 1986, he alleged that some community centres in West Belfast were fronts for the IRA. He said that he had written to Nicholas Scott calling for funds to these community centres to be stopped. Feeney continued:

> 'I have no doubt whatsoever that the Conway Mill is a front for considerable enterprise by Sinn Féin and the Provos and they

moved in there because it's in the Enterprise Zone, to benefit from favourable tax and rates.'

Like Douglas Hurd, Feeney produced no evidence for this claim and refused publicly to substantiate it. Feeney's Party never publicly refuted his allegation.

Development at the Mill was therefore crippled by lack of government funding. Funds to ACE workers were refused; the DED went so far as to impose a boycott on all ACE workers from entering the Mill. Potential investment through LEDU and the Enterprise Zone was axed; existing tenants at the Mill were refused grants and told that unless they went elsewhere they would continue to be refused grants; others who wished to go into the Mill were told that they would be refused grants if they did so. The education initiative suffered also, with Rupert Stanley College withdrawing its teachers. Government pressure was applied to organisations such as the Workers' Educational Association to have them boycott the Mill under pain of financial loss.

On November 2, 1987. Mr. Jim Marshall MP asked the Secretary of State for Northern Ireland about organisations which had been informed of the possible loss of government funding for ACE workers or other projects because of their present or proposed use of the Conway Mill; what action, he asked, were such organisations advised to take if they wished to retain such funding? Mr. John Stanley for the NIO replied:

> 'Three organisations were informed of the possible loss of government funding because of their use of the Conway Mill facilities ... The organisations were advised to re-locate.'

Political Vetting

Writing in 1976, a rising star in the *Sunday Times'* firmament, Chris Ryder, attacked a number of community enterprises in West Belfast which went under the collective name of the Andersonstown Co-op. Formed in 1974 by a number of ex-internees, it was not, he said, what it appeared to be. To the innocent observer it was a way for ex-internees to guarantee themselves secure employment. But Ryder knew better.

> 'Knowing they will never persuade the Catholics to vote for them at the ballot box, the Provos have resorted to controlling essential community needs ... Military intelligence analysts believe that the Provisionals could one day use their power over the supply of vital necessities, like food, to force the Catholic community to support them. "Particularly in the event of a doomsday situation between Catholics and Protestants", says a senior security advisor. "The Provos could say: "If you want bread or milk for your family, guard this street or drive this car·" The Provos' operations, besides giving them influence, also provide a huge cash flow to finance expansion and the pursuit of military objectives.'[3]

In short, Ryder's opposition was based on the allegation that such enterprises were a front providing both legitimacy and funds to 'terrorists'.

Ryder went on to consider the West Belfast Taxi Association in the same vein. At the same time, as we have seen, the government was trying its best to force that Association out of business. As well as the financial considerations in relation to Citybus profits, the government had reached the same conclusion about the taxis as had Ryder. The difference was this: for all the power of an influential British newspaper to damage the reputation and business of the Andersonstown Co-op, Ryder's broadside was nothing more than sensationalist. But when the government reached the same paranoid conclusion it was in a position to act directly against community enterprises. In the case of the taxis many tactics were tried.

The allegation of local development enterprises acting as fronts providing legitimacy and funds for 'terrorists' was not publicly voiced by government in the case of the Whiterock Industrial Estate. But there is little doubt that such a belief made it easier for the state to steamroll over a perfectly viable economic initiative in order to build an army fort. When some of the people who had been involved in the Industrial Estate moved on to their next project, the Conway Mill, they found that, after an initial honeymoon period, their development was blocked just as ruthlessly and comprehensively as that of the taxi association before them. Again the reasoning was that the Mill was a front for the IRA.

The difference this time was that the government came out into the open with its allegations. Ten years after Ryder had written his piece Douglas Hurd spoke in almost identical terms of the need to curtail any initiatives which would contribute to the support of 'terrorists'. Hurd's allegations were even more vague and unsubstantiated than Ryder's. At least in the case of the *Sunday Times* article the manager of Andersonstown Co-op was able to sue successfully for libel. The Trustees of Conway Mill and the ACE workers who were sacked had no such compensation.

The Conway Mill was not alone. After Hurd's Commons statement in 1985 seven groups, all of them in Nationalist areas, two in the West Belfast constituency, lost their funding. They were: Dove House, Shantallow Tenants' Association and Gobnascale Community Centre (all in Derry), the Conway Mill Education Project, the Conway Mill crèche, the MacAirt Naomhscoil and Twinbrook Tenants' and Community Association (all in Belfast). After a sustained campaign against the government decision, Dove House had its funding restored.

It must be stressed repeatedly that the government produced no proof of links between these groups—including two crèches—and the IRA. In the absence of such proof it can only be assumed, in the words of Peter Archer, former Labour Party spokesperson on Northern Ireland, that the seven projects were being punished 'for the politics of the community in which they operate'.[4] Or, to quote the conclusion of a public inquiry held at the Conway Mill in May 1988:

> 'If a project is a genuine community-based initiative creating jobs and providing a service for the community, and if its management and accounts are in order, it is utterly unacceptable that it should not receive ACE funding on the basis of its alleged political associations. Projects should be considered on their own merit, rather than whether or not they are politically acceptable to the government of the day.'[5]

Footnotes

1. *Belfast Urban Area Plan: Review of Transportation Strategy*, Belfast, Department of the Environment, 1978.
2. Letter from Denis Myles, Belfast Enterprise Zone, to Fr. Desmond Wilson, May 1984.
3. Ryder, C., 'Belfast's New God-fathers', *Sunday Times* 22/8/76.
4. Quoted in McKnight, M., 'Political Vetting of Community Groups', in *The Nationalist Nightmare: Report of a Conference on the Effects of the Hillsborough Agreement*, Belfast: 1987.
5. Quoted in Barron, S., 'NIO holds all the ACEs', *Fortnight* 264, July/August 1988, p. 6.

11.

Conclusion: Work for West Belfast

The purpose of this final chapter is twofold: to present the conclusions reached in the course of the study, and to make specific proposals as to how the task of bringing jobs to West Belfast might begin.

The proposals are specific and are presented for the careful consideration of government, statutory agencies, voluntary organisations, community groups, the churches, *Obair* itself, and others concerned about the unemployment problem. It would be presumptuous to describe these proposals as *the* way forward; they are offered as a contribution to an economic development debate which has been underway in the constituency for some time. There is something in the proposals for each of these audiences to consider with a view to seeing how they can make their specific contribution to the economic revival of West Belfast. Moreover, the proposals are the basis for our final and over-arching *proposal that a task force be set up immediately to deal with the economic redevelopment of West Belfast.*

The Decline of West Belfast

This report began by examining how employment opportunities in West Belfast have changed since the heyday of industrial capitalism in the north east of Ireland. At the beginning of this century half of Belfast's Catholic women workers, the vast majority of whom lived in the west of the city, were employed in textile production. Domestic service was another major source of employment. Although Catholic men were also employed in the linen mills, they were more likely to be working as unskilled labourers, in transport, the building industry, or not working at all. At the same time, Protestant workers were heavily represented in the more skilled, better paid and relatively secure occupations in the shipbuilding, engineering and chemical industries.

By the onset of the current recession, almost three-quarters of the jobs on which the area depended had disappeared. Attempts to broaden the North's narrow and declining industrial base largely by-passed West Belfast and, but for the expansion of public sector employment associated with the growth of the welfare state, the area would have become an economic wasteland. Thus a post-war regional strategy which favoured predominantly Protestant growth centres and ignored

West Belfast was partly compensated by an increase in employment in education, health and, latterly, housing. The expansion of the Royal Victoria Hospital in the heart of the constituency became a particularly important source of employment.

As Chapter 7 showed, West Belfast did acquire new manufacturing employment for a brief period in the second half of the 1970s but this was a short-lived development. As the recession took hold, the new companies, and most of the remaining old ones, closed down. Today's pattern was set: very high rates of unemployment for men, offset by some public sector work and self-employment, and an unknown volume of emigration. For women, the pattern is one of high, though concealed, unemployment, but with an increasingly part-time involvement in the public sector and in private sector services and distribution.

What's the Problem

The pursuit of monetarism has served to accelerate the trend towards unemployment in the 1980s for reasons outlined in Chapter 3. Monetarism means an end to the post-war commitment to full employment—in effect, the eradication of the right to work from the political agenda. Yet the government's approach has been selective and uneven. West Belfast people are acutely aware of the contradictions of monetarism in the context of the North. On the one hand they see the relentless decline of their own area; on the other they see continuing public subsidy of the shipyard and Shorts on the other side of the city. No-one we have spoken to wants these companies to collapse, and with them, the remnants of the North's industrial base—quite the contrary. But it is the sense of unequal treatment that matters and angers.

The continuing attack on the public sector which a monetarist economic policy involves threatens to erode the last remaining large-scale source of employment in West Belfast. As it is, work at the Royal Victoria Hospital is being casualized: ancillary jobs are increasingly part-time with fewer and fewer hours being worked. Similarly, employment in the schools has declined in respect to cleaners, caterers and teachers. Expenditure on building in West Belfast, whether roads or houses, has been propped up by European Community receipts as Chapter 8 indicates. Nevertheless, building work remains intermittent and insecure.

The results of a decade of monetarism are very obvious in West Belfast. The widening of inequalities detailed in Chapter 4 is most evident in terms of cuts in social security entitlements and the consequential growth of personal debt and the use of enforced debt recovery. The proliferation of second-hand clothes shops and 'cheap meat' stores provides some of the more visible signs of the low levels of household incomes. The very high rates of unemployment throughout West Belfast, discussed in Chapter 6, are associated with a wide range of personal consequences from depression to suicide, from heart disease to premature death. Unemployment is also linked to some types of law-breaking, in particular involving young people. Whatever the arguments about the directness of such associations, unemployment unmistakably means enduring life on a low income, sometimes for years on end—on a weekly sum which those at the other end of the income scale would hardly think twice about spending on a single meal. The implications for the children of West Belfast are clear: because of low household incomes, more than half of them are being reared on inadequate diets, with all that this implies in terms of physical, mental and social underdevelopment. Generations of children are being condemned to inferiority long before they enter the trial of school examinations, let alone the competition for employment.

Such evidence flies in the face of what we are told about the nature of unemployment by the pedlars of Victorian values. They would have us believe that unemployment is essentially a cultural problem: its solution lies in a revolution of ideas and attitudes amongst the unemployed themselves, and in the triumph of enterprise over dependency. As Chapter 4 argued, this notion amounts to little more than social prejudice against unemployed people. A more forceful argument, which was also examined in Chapter 4, is that much of the unemployment in the North and in predominantly Catholic areas such as West Belfast is directly attributable to the IRA's campaign. The consensus amongst leading economists is quite clear on this point. Yes, the IRA's actions have been costly, but it is political instability and the lack of consensus amongst politicians, rather than the armed conflict as such, which prevents foreign investment and inhibits economic development.

Chapter 5 outlined the arguments about why Catholic men are more than twice as likely to be unemployed as Protestant men and identified three key processes. The most readily identifiable of these involves acts of discrimination by employers, both intended and unintended, in the hiring and firing of workers. Many commentators believe that discrimination in this conventional sense has all but died out and some suggest that past claims of discrimination have been grossly exaggerated. Such views have little by way of convincing evidence to support them. The second process discussed in Chapter 5 relates to intimidation and the third is to do with the 'structural discrimination' engendered by the history of the location of new jobs and job losses. The recently published White Paper on Fair Employment contains only one principle to which there appears to be serious commitment on the part of government—that of ensuring that all workers are hired on the basis of individual merit. As such, the White Paper's proposals will probably have limited effects on employer personnel practices, even less effect on the various forms of intimidation and will make no impact at all on structural discrimination. To do otherwise would be an unwarranted interference with that other principle close to the heart of government—free market inequality.

The purpose of the White Paper seems to be to convince existing and potential American investors that real progress is being made towards fair employment and that government policy supercedes the MacBride principles. To American eyes the MacBride principles embody traditional concepts of equality, as well as guidelines for redressing current inequalities which have become widely accepted over the past two decades. Americans thus find it hard to comprehend the British government's opposition to MacBride. All the government appears to be concerned about is that if people have heard of the MacBride principles they should know to be against them.

The government's approach to the unemployment differential between Catholics and Protestants is, therefore, conditioned by its opposition to the campaign to get American investors to adopt a principled approach to employment equality in the North of Ireland. It is also heavily constrained by an indvidualistic approach to the unemployment problem as a whole.

But perhaps the most effective way in which the unemployment problem has been masked is through the presentation of the official unemployment statistics, looked at in Chapter 6. After 24 changes to the unemployment count, these statistics now seriously understate the size of the problem and provide misleading assessments of trends regarding, for instance, changes in the scale of female, youth and long-term unemployment.

The State's Response to Unemployment

In addition to analysing how West Belfast lost out on job promotion in the past, Chapters 7 and 8 presented evidence of the treatment of the area in the 1980s. In the mid-1980s, companies in West Belfast were receiving a mere 1% of the IDB's total grant aid budget. The IDB's actions demonstrate a complete lack of strategic thinking in relation to severely depressed areas such as West Belfast. Similarly, LEDU lacks a strategic role, measuring its performance simply in terms of nominal jobs created and the cost of those jobs. It provides no information about where it creates jobs or on the social distribution of those jobs. Recently, LEDU has had a higher profile in West Belfast, although it seems to have been drawn into reinforcing government political directives as to which local initiatives to support and which to reject.

When it comes to international aid, the record is somewhat better. It is not entirely clear what employment or other benefits will flow from the International Fund's investments in West Belfast, but it *is* clear that the Fund lacks independence. There is strong evidence that the International Fund has in effect become another branch of the British government. Indeed, this propensity to control international resources has generated some friction between the European Community and the government, Europe being the other major source of international aid.

While it appears that the European Community does seek to take a strategic role in relation to economic development, the spatial effects of this intervention do not appear to be monitored. As Chapter 8 showed, however, we have been able to determine that in the mid-1980s West Belfast industry received 2% of the industry allocations for the whole of the North which came from the Regional Development Fund. West Belfast got 6% of the North's infrastructure allocations from the same fund, as far as we have been able to determine. There is no readily available information on the employment effects of European aid. We do not know in any detail how much new work has been created and who got the jobs.

Over the past ten years much criticism has been levelled at government training policies and special employment measures, and the co-operation of participants, trainers, employers, sponsors and trade unions has been tested to breaking point. Chapter 9 showed that the schemes have developed at an alarming pace, to the point where serious skills training is low down the priorities list. Of much greater concern to government is the coercion of the unemployed through an American-style system of 'workfare' under which people must work for their social security benefits. At the same time, the organisation and curricula of the various schemes have moved further and further away from the needs of the unemployed and are gradually being adapted to the political goals of conservatism. In the context of West Belfast, these developments are evident in the way in which the churches have been chosen as the main sponsors of ACE posts. Whatever the presumed effects of this policy, the deficiences of what will soon become the Adult Training Programme will remain.

It is clear from Chapter 10 that the government's boost to church involvement in employment and training schemes is operating in tandem with a policy which denies resources to projects not under church control. More specifically, for many years the government has put obstacles in the way of a range of attempts by local people to generate employment on the grounds that their schemes were in some way linked to the IRA. Typically, the projects have shown great enterprise and initiative, qualities much lauded by the present government. A creche, an education scheme and a nursery school are amongst those projects which have recently been effected by the denial or withdrawal of funds. On several occasions, the government has been pressed in the House of Commons to explain its policy more fully. On every such occasion questioners have simply been referred back to Douglas Hurd's original statement quoted in Chapter 10. In none of these cases has the government claimed that a project lacked merit. No evidence of 'paramilitary links' has ever been produced nor has the government sought fit to define what it means by 'links'. The British government's commitment to the merit principle in the case of equality of opportunity for individuals stands in sharp contrast to its denial of the merit principle in relation to groups trying to provide desperately needed local employment and services.

This process of 'political vetting' as it has become known not only affects resources under the direct control of government agencies but it also affects international aid as we saw in Chapter 8. The International Fund turned down an application by Conway Mill because it had been directly advised that to do otherwise would not be consistent with the British government's policies and priorities. The parallels between this political direction of international aid and the powers being formalised by the South African government under the Orderly Internal Politics Bill are quite striking. This Bill is designed to ban international aid to groups assisting the victims of apartheid and will mean, for example, that European Community funds will have to be channelled through organisations approved by the South African government.

Developing Work

Having read this report, no-one should be in any doubt about the severity of the unemployment problem in West Belfast. Unemployment rates in excess of 50% are commonplace in many parts of the constituency. More than a tenth of all those in the North who have been out of work for more than a year live in West Belfast. The area also has an excessive share of youth unemployment, whether the government chooses to regard those on training schemes as 'in work' or not. Women in West Belfast are less likely to be in full-time paid employment than women in other areas. One ward in the constituency has eight times as much unemployment as the Stormont ward in which government makes most of its decisions.

In Chapter 6 we made a conservative estimate that 18,000 jobs were needed in the constituency to provide employment for all those wanting and seeking work. During the preparation of this report we have often been asked what is our estimate of the investment required to bring full employment to the constituency. Before suggesting a figure, it should be pointed out that a great deal is already being spent in the area on denying the right to work. Unemployment costs money in benefits and lost taxes; using conservative assumptions, we estimate the direct costs of unemployment in the constituency to be in the region of £118m each year. But it is also expensive in terms of additional strains on health and social services, in terms of the costs of anti-social activities such as vandalism and other less quantifiable consequences.

But creating 18,000 jobs could cost more than this in the short-term. At IDB rates, the figure would be around £425m; at LEDU rates, about £112m. Using a mixture of public and private sector strategies, and large and small projects, an investment exceeding £240m, or £48m every year for a five year period, suggests itself. It is not for us to suggest the exact source of finances of such magnitude. However, we would insist that money for the revitalisation of West Belfast should *not* be acquired through the disadvantaging of other working class areas in the North. We would also suggest that the sum specified above is slight compared to the amount spent every year by the British government on defence, or the windfall given to the rich in last April's budget.

But to some extent such figures are arbitrary. The important point is a political one: the resources which the government recently promised for *North and West* Belfast pale into insignificance alongside the real scale of investment required for the West Belfast constituency alone.

The sort of economic 'new deal' suggested by these figures is very far from the minds of government advisers and quite the reverse of present policies. The past decade of monetarism is draining West Belfast of resources. As the fanfare sounds for new resources coming into the area, other government policies are taking money out of the area. We have not had the information or resources to draw up a list of recent gains and losses, but we can confidently claim that cuts in the value of social security benefits since 1980 alone amount to more than the value of the government's latest initiative.

Much of the analysis in this report suggests that little meaningful progress on job creation can be made while a government heavily influenced by radical right-wing economic and social policies remains in power. Certainly a more Keynesian and socially egalitarian approach might be expected of any future Labour government, an approach which could bring about significantly improved job prospects. But whatever the economic constraints which would face Labour within Britain and internationally, such a government would still have to contend with two major factors shaping the North of Ireland's economy and the position of West Belfast within it. Firstly, the lack of political stability imposes heavy constraints on economic development, not just because foreign capital is reluctant to locate in the North, but for many other economic and social reasons such as the problems of retaining and attracting the most skilled, educated and motivated workers, or losses to tourism. Secondly, and a reflection of the political divisions, there is the problem of the historical subordination of West Belfast and in particular its Catholic inhabitants. Through a combination of structural, political and labour market discrimination, large sections of the constituency are being denied access to work and decent living standards. In effect, many people have been permanently excluded from any hold on reasonable social and material expectations; a class of non-citizens has been created.

Realistically, the future looks bleak. This has not deterred commentators from speculating about the future of work or formulating guidelines for the development of the economy. A number of scenarios crop up in such discussions. Perhaps the most pessimistic of these suggests that work, particularly in 'post-industrial' societies, is gradually becoming more scarce under the impact of new technologies and the contraction of manufacturing industry. Coupled with market-oriented economic policies, the decline of work is generating a growing group of permanently or frequently unemployed people, with sharp social divisions between them and those who still have jobs. A slightly less pessimistic scenario suggests that those excluded from work could form the basis of a new 'leisure class', or at least may be persuaded that life without work is tolerable.

A third possibility implies a more interventionist role for the state in the distribution of the work that does exist. This might include, for example, more job-sharing schemes, extending educational opportunities, an increase in the use of paid breaks from work (whether for parenting, study or training), banning overtime and the possession of more than one job, and even the introduction of a restriction on the number of hours it is permissible to work. Clearly, the redistribution of work implies a fairer spread of the income and status which work provides.

All of these possibilities seem to assume two things: firstly, that 'work' means paid employment (or self-employment) and secondly, that there is a shortage of work. Regarding the first argument, an enormous amount of work is carried out for no payment at all, especially by women in the home, or by friends and neighbours on a 'tit-for-tat' basis. The formal economy of paid employment would operate far less smoothly in the absence of the domestic labour largely undertaken by women. The second idea, that there is a scarcity of work, is only seriously supported by those who lack the vision to see what work needs to be done and could be done in an area like West Belfast. What such people usually mean is they cannot see a way of securing the necessary resources. The acceptance of a broad concept of work, which includes work in the home and local neighbourhood, as well as jobs which need doing for the general benefit of an area or specific groups within it, would present a challenge to the way in which work is currently valued and rewarded. It also implies a redistribution of resources from current sources of paid employment towards those activities, such as child care, which are typically not paid for.

Notions such as the redistribution and redefinition of work and its associated benefits may seem idealistic and fanciful, but they only seem so because of the dismal and dogged pursuit of the first scenario outlined above, and the support for this approach within the upper echelons of the civil service. The straightjacket of contemporary economic policies and job creation programmes forces the discussion of economic development into a narrow debate of public versus private sector, of transnational enterprise versus local enterprise and of large versus small-scale projects. Of more use is the growing discussion of economic 'linkages' and integration, both within the North and between the North and South. This involves an attempt to target developmental resources on particular sectors of industry and to encourage links between companies, getting firms to provide equipment, goods and services which would otherwise be bought in from Britain.

The long-term aim must obviously be to resuscitate the industrial base and inevitably this will involve a mixture of foreign and indigenous capital (private and public). As we have said, to be successful it will involve a considerably more energetic and imaginative role on the part of state agencies than is possible under the present regime. In the short-term, there must be discussion to define the social objectives of economic development in order to clarify the goals which will replace the moribund creed of monetarism.

In our view, the end of unemployment and the right to meaningful work must be in the forefront of this discussion. This does not mean the provision of jobs at any price. Of central interest ought to be the type of work created, the conditions under which that work is carried out and the nature of the products or service. The notion of 'ethical investment' could be useful in this context. Ethical investors choose, for example, to avoid tobacco manufacturers, or the arms trade, or those transnational companies who abuse their workers in South Korea or South Africa. Investment criteria might also be related to environmental concerns or an employer's policy with regard to various forms of discrimination. Such a discussion, therefore, would be as concerned with the nuts and bolts of how to create worthwhile employment opportunities as with the fairness of where jobs were located and which groups benefited.

How to make areas such as West Belfast a priority for economic development should also be high on the agenda. As we have sought to emphasize, the reasons for West Belfast's unemployment problem involve a complex history of economic decline, political discrimination and social exclusion. This economic history is further complicated by nearly twenty years of armed conflict and political instability of such intensity that decision-making about the economy and other matters is highly centralised. It is our belief that the promotion of social justice in the form of meaningful employment can contribute to the development of political progress. Indeed an end to the conflict is difficult to imagine without a substantial reduction in the prevailing economic inequalities. To this end, we suggest that all those agencies, government and non-government, which are involved in West Belfast, or which have responsibilities which mean they *ought* to be involved, should closely examine their decisions and actions with regard to any employment/unemployment consequences. The effect on the local labour market should become a routine concern of all involved. A second requirement for progress is that government agencies directly concerned with job promotion should become much more involved in the constituency. This means having a presence in the area, getting to know the people and their problems and aspirations, consulting with all shades of opinion on the area's needs and beginning a dialogue on the way forward.

Conclusions

On the basis of the above arguments and evidence we have reached four major conclusions.

1. West Belfast's decline is long-term. Consequently any *serious* consideration of the reversal of that decline must also be long-term. Fundamental changes are required and can only result from a planned strategic approach to the area. For too long the area has been virtually ignored by government job creation agencies. The economic revival of the area must become a priority on the political agenda of government.
2. Very high rates of unemployment such as are found in West Belfast are not just the product of long-term decline. They result from what we have called structural discrimination, as well as from individual acts of discrimination against Catholics, and intimidation in the workplace. These processes have combined to make it difficult for West Belfast Catholics to get jobs outside the area.
3. Monetarism has contributed to the speeding up of the decline of West Belfast. Specifically, monetarism has little to offer in terms of solving one of the greatest social problems of the area, namely, unemployment at rates frequently well in excess of 50%. An interventionist strategy is a prerequisite for the revival of West Belfast.
4. Current government assistance to the area, minimal though it may be, is far too narrowly targeted. The concentration of training and other resources in organisations which are seen to be controlled by the churches is wasteful of the talents and energies of many people in the area. It is wrong that local initiatives are being deprived of resources either because they lack church involvement or on the grounds of unsubstantiated allegations that they are linked to the IRA.

The Task Force

The perspective we have taken in this report is unashamedly pluralist. It envisages a mixture of strategies—private sector, public sector and community-based—to develop work in West Belfast. With this perspective in mind, we have drawn up a list of specific points for immediate consideration.

Two preliminary caveats must be sounded. Firstly, although we have attempted in one sense to avoid issues of UK-wide policy such as taxation or social security, our criticisms of monetarism and support for a planned strategy for the revival of West Belfast demand a change in current British government priorities. Secondly, a decade and a half of relatively non-accountable centralised administration in the North of

Ireland has resulted in government departments being remarkably closed to criticism, even criticism of a positive nature. Hence we believe that a new forum should be established which would represent the willingness of government to prioritise West Belfast. This forum is needed to encourage positive criticism, imaginative suggestions and the joint efforts of government and local people to formulate a strategy for the economic revitalisation of the area.

If the provision of meaningful employment for West Belfast is to be given the priority it deserves, a special task force, publicly accountable, properly resourced and including a broad range of local people, should be established to draw up a programme involving relevant timetables and deadlines to develop the area and reverse the current situation.

The setting up of the task force would be the first act in showing a serious commitment to tackling the problems of the area by giving them the priority they deserve. It would signal to the residents of the constituency that there is a political will to revitalise the area.

Specific Proposals

On the basis of the arguments presented in this report and of the conclusions reached, we are putting forward a number of specific proposals for the consideration of the task force.

Monitoring and Information

1. An alternative index of unemployment, along the lines of the London-based Unemployment Unit's index, should be produced to replace the now discredited official statistics.
2. The employment effects of IDB and LEDU assistance should be routinely monitored so that it is clear which sections of the labour force are benefiting.
3. The social distribution of job losses could be better understood.
4. Attempts should be made to find out more about emigration from the North of Ireland.
5. Contributors of international aid should monitor its distribution and employment effects to ensure that West Belfast receives resources commensurate with the employment needs of the area.

Job Promotion

6. The IDB and others involved in attempts to attract industry to the North should seek to raise the profile of West Belfast. This includes how the area is represented to potential investors as well as the policy of differential grants for areas of high unemployment. This differential could be substantially increased.
7. As in the 1970s, the IDB should establish manufacturing projects in West Belfast. These could be developed with the assistance of scientists and engineers, particularly those working in declining

industries, who could be encouraged to devise socially useful technologies/products.

8. The DED should fund several 'think-tanks' of local people, backed up by specialist resources, to identify services and products which may form the basis of viable businesses, whether these are run on co-operative principles or as profit-maximising enterprises.
9. Efforts must be made to curtail the emigration of highly skilled, educated and motivated people by providing opportunities for these people to use their talents in the social and economic development of areas such as West Belfast. One idea, similar to the think-tank concept, would be to pump resources into product research and development on the sort of scale which has enabled Japanese industry to become so technically advanced.

Training

10. The centralising of training and employment schemes is a recipe for rigidity and uniformity. Innovation and flexibility would be better achieved through a wider range of providers.
11. Those engaged in the provision of employment and training schemes should do what they can to resist a curriculum geared to a narrow concept of employers' needs. This type of 'training', especially without jobs to follow, is demeaning (and increasingly coercive) and should be replaced by a broader concept of training for social advance. This includes the acquisition of specific skills as well as continuing education, as part of an employment development strategy.
12. Efforts should be made to challenge the gender stereotyping in training schemes.
13. The development of further education facilities should include the targeting of employment development, providing a forum for discussion, specific business skills training, information resources and access to new technology.

Ending Discrimination

14. The costly campaign against the MacBride principles should be ended and the funds diverted towards investigating and preventing intimidation in the workplace.
15. Targets should be established for reducing both unemployment itself and the unemployment differential between Catholics and Protestants.
16. The current practice of 'political vetting' should cease. No group, project or initiative should be deprived of funds without a full and proper explanation, and a right of appeal.
17. Contributors of international aid should seek to develop criteria for the allocation of funds which are independent of government policies.

Reversing the Cuts

18. Any future plans for the Royal Victoria Hospital should be considered in the light of *expanding* its importance as an employer of West Belfast people.
19. Housing Executive cuts should be restored and the budget increased in order to accelerate the redevelopment of anti-social housing (*eg* Divis, Unity), the improvement of substandard dwellings and the refurbishment of existing houses. As a matter of policy, this work should employ people from within the area.
20. More resources need to be channelled to the schools to facilitate better maintenance and upkeep, the provision of wholesome meals, smaller class sizes and more books and equipment, including computers.
21. There is an immediate need for more workers to be employed in the administration of social security in the area, in order to relieve pressures generated by the introduction of Income Support.

Developing Services

22. Special projects (using additional resources) involving a range of specialists should be established to address the short- and long-term personal effects of unemployment, and to provide appropriate services.
23. Health care remains underdeveloped. Special efforts should be made to encourage doctors to establish practices in West Belfast.
24. Health services need to be developed which are in tune with the problems faced by people in the area. Provision for women is especially lacking.
25. More support is required for initiatives from local people and voluntary organisations dealing with young people caught up in anti-social behaviour. Crime prevention initiatives of this kind might be linked with involving young people in the provision of services, facilities and leisure of their own design and making. Self-build single persons' accommodation is an idea worth pursuing.
26. The most serious shortage of social provision is in relation to child care. Parents cannot go out to work if there is nowhere for their children to be properly cared for. Such facilities should be generously resourced and be available on a flexible basis, not just for those with jobs, but for anyone who needs time to do unpaid work or who simply needs a break from the stresses of parenting. A wide range of organisations could act as providers of such services. This proposal demands a large investment in recognition that West Belfast's future is its children.

Documentary Sources

Action on Debt, *Sticking the Knife in: Debt and Debt Collection in Northern Ireland*, Belfast, 1980.

Additionality of European Community Funds: Submission to Assembly Finance and Personnel Committee, Belfast: Northern Ireland Economic Council, Paper 2, February 1983.

Allen, S. *et al* (eds.), *The Experience of Unemployment*, London: Macmillan, 1986.

Andersonstown News.

An Phoblacht/Republican News.

Ashton, D. N., *Unemployment under Capitalism: The Sociology of British and American Labour Markets*, Brighton: Wheatsheaf Books, 1986.

Barron, S., 'NIO holds all the ACEs', *Fortnight* 264, July/August 1988.

Belfast Areas of Special Social Need, Report by Project Team. Belfast: H.M.S.O., 1976.

Belfast Bulletin.

Belfast Household Survey, 1978, Belfast: Northern Ireland Housing Executive, 1979.

Belfast Telegraph.

Belfast Urban Area Plan: Review of Transportation Strategy, Belfast, Department of the Environment, 1978.

Beveridge, W. H., *Full Employment in a Free Society*, London: Allen and Unwin, 1944.

Blackman, T., 'Community Action and the Economy', *Scope*, October 1986, pp. 14-15.

Bleakley, D., *Trade Union Beginnings in Belfast and District*, unpublished M.A. Thesis, Belfast: Queen's University, 1955.

Boyd, A., *Holy War in Belfast*, Tralee: Anvil Books, 1969.

Brown, C. and Gay, P., *Racial Discrimination: 17 Years after the Act*, London: Policy Studies Institute, 1985.

Budge, I. and O'Leary, C., *Belfast: Approach to Crisis*, London: Macmillan 1973.

Canning, D., Moore, B., and Rhodes, J., 'Economic Growth: Problems and Prospects', in Teague, P., (ed.) *Beyond the Rhetoric: Politics, the Economy and Social Policy in Northern Ireland*, London: Lawrence and Wishart, 1987.

Christine, K., *et. al.*, 'Community Development and the Local Economy, Part 1', *Scope*, February 1987, pp. 6-8

Christine, K., *et. al.*, 'Community Development and the Local Economy, Part 2', *Scope*, March 1987, pp. 14-16

Cole-Hamilton, I. and Lang, T., *Tightening Belts: A Report on the Impact of Poverty on Food*, London: London Food Commission, 1986.

Community Research Services, *A Social and Economic Profile of the Households in the Lower Shankill*, Belfast: Centre for the Unemployed, 1988.

Compton, P. 'Demographic and geographical aspects of the unemployment differential between Protestants and Roman Catholics in Northern Ireland', in P. Compton (ed.), *The Contemporary Population of Northern Ireland and Population-Related Issues*, Belfast: Queen's University, 1981.

Darby, J. and Morris, G., *Intimidation in Housing*, Belfast: Northern Ireland Community Relations Commission, February 1974.

Department of Community Medicine, Eastern Health and Social Services Board, *A Picture of Health?*, Belfast, 1988.

Department of Economic Development, *A Step in the Right Direction: Youth Training Programme Review and Plan*, 1984.

Devlin, P., *Yes We Have No Bananas: Outdoor Relief in Belfast 1920-39*, Belfast: Blackstaff Press, 1981.

Doherty, P., 'MacBride effort: US map keeps on getting darker', *Fortnight* No. 264, July/August 1988, pp. 11-12.

Donaldson, P., *A Question of Economics*, Harmondsworth: Penguin Books, 1985.

Economic Implications for Northern Ireland and the Republic of Ireland of Recent Developments in the European Community, Northern Ireland Economic Council/National Economic and Science Council, February 1988.

Economic Strategy: Industrial Development, Northern Ireland Economic Council Report Number 60, August 1986.

Evason, E., *On the Edge: a study of poverty and long-term unemployment in Northern Ireland*, London: Child Poverty Action Group, 1985.

Fair Employment Agency, *A Final Report of the Fair Employment Agency for Northern Ireland into the Employment Practices of the Northern Ireland Electricity Service*, Belfast, 1982.

Fair Employment Agency, *Engineering Investigation and Report*, Belfast, n.d.

Fair Employment in Northern Ireland, London: HMSO, Cm. 380, 1988.

Gaffikin, F. and Morrissey, M., 'Community Action and the Economy', *Scope*, April 1986, pp. 6-10.

Gaffikin, F. and Morrissey, M., 'The Local Economy: Development in a Changing World', *Scope*, May 1986, pp. 12-15.

Gaffikin, F. and Morrissey, M., 'The Economy: a Popular Alternative', *Scope*, June 1986, pp. 14-17.

Gaffikin, F. and Morrissey, M., 'Economic Strategy in Northern Ireland: a Reply to Discussion (Part 1)', *Scope*, June 1987, pp. 6-8.

Gaffikin, F. and Morrissey, M., 'Economic Strategy in Northern

Ireland: a Reply to Discussion (Part Two)', *Scope*, July/August 1987, pp. 16-18.

Gaffikin, F. and Morrissey, M., 'Bringing Cheer to a Depressed Economy', *Local Economy* 2(1), 1987.

Gaffikin, F. and Morrissey, M., 'Popular Planning in Northern Ireland—A Viable Alternative?' *Local Economy* 2(2), 1987.

Gibson, N., 'Political and Economic Integration', in D. Rea (ed.) *Political Co-operation in Divided Societies*, Dublin: Gill and Macmillan, 1983.

Gillespie, N., *The Vital Statistics: Shankill Employment Report*, Belfast: Shankill Community Council, 1983.

Greater Belfast Area Household Survey, 1985. Belfast: Northern Ireland Housing Executive, 1986.

Gribbon, S., *Edwardian Belfast: A Social Profile*, Belfast: Appletree Press 1983.

Guardian.

Hansard.

Heatley, F., 'Community Relations and the Religious Geography, 1800-1860,' in J. C. Beckett *et al.*, *Belfast: The Making of the City*, Belfast: Appletree Press, 1983.

Hepburn, A. C., *Employment and Religion in Belfast 1901-1971*, Belfast: Fair Employment Agency, 1982.

Hill, M., 'Government Responses to Unemployment', in M. Loney, D. Boswell and J. Clarke (eds), *Social Policy and Social Welfare*, Milton Keynes, Open University Press, 1983, pp. 241-254.

Howe, L., 'Unemployment: historical aspects of data collection and the black economy in Belfast', Belfast: Queen's University (mimeo), 1985.

Howe, L., 'Unemployment, Doing the Double and Labour Markets in Belfast', in Curtin, C. and Wilson, T., (eds) *Ireland from Below: Social Change and Local Communities*, Dublin: Gill and Macmillan, 1988.

Independent.

Investor's Chronicle.

Irish News.

Isles, K. and Cuthbert, N., *An Economic Survey of Northern Ireland*, Belfast: H.M.S.O., 1957.

Jenkins, R. and Harding, P., Informal Economic Activity in Northern Ireland: A Review of the Literature, PPRU Occasional Paper No. 15, Belfast: Department of Finance and Personnel, 1988.

Jones, E., *A Social Geography of Belfast*, London: Oxford University Press, 1960.

Kelvin, P. and Jarrett, J., *Unemployment: Its Social Psychological Effects*, Cambridge: Cambridge University Press, 1985.

Keynes, J. M. *General Theory of Employment, Interest and Money*, London: Macmillan, 1936.

Low Pay Review.
Lawson, N., *Tax Reform: the Government's Record*, London: Conservative Political Centre, 1988.
McAteer, G., *Down the Falls*, Belfast: Falls Community Council, 1983.
McCullagh, M. 'Youth Unemployment and the Ideology of Control', in Curtin, C., Kelly, M. and O'Dowd, L. (eds), *Culture and Ideology in Ireland*, Galway: Galway University Press, 1984.
McCullagh, M., 'The Social Construction of Unemployment', in Clancy, P. *et al* (eds.), *Ireland: A Sociological Profile*. Dublin: Institute of Public Administration, 1986.
McKnight, M., 'Political Vetting of Community Groups', in *The Nationalist Nightmare: Report of a Conference on the Effects of the Hillsborough Agreement*, Belfast, 1987.
McMahon, G. 'Ireland and Britain—Minimum Wages in the Poor Nations of Europe', *Low Pay Review* No. 30, 1987, pp. 13-20.
Mallie, E., 'The Provos' Resurgence: there's more to come', *Fortnight* 265, September 1988, p. 7.
Moon, J. and Richardson, J., *Unemployment in the UK*, Aldershot: Gower, 1985.
Munck, R. and Rolston, B., *Belfast in the Thirties: an Oral History*, Belfast: Blackstaff Press, 1987.
Neill, W. 'Optimism Versus Realism—Economic Development in Northern Ireland: A Reply to Mike Morrissey and Frank Gaffikin', *Local Economy* 2(4), 1988, pp. 314-322.
New Ireland Forum, *The Cost of Violence arising from the Northern Ireland Crisis since 1969*, Dublin: Stationery Office, 1983.
News Letter.
Northern Ireland Census, 1981.
Northern Ireland Housing Executive, *Greater Belfast Area Household Survey 1985*, Belfast, 1986.
Observer.
O'Dowd, L., 'Regional Policy', in L. O'Dowd, B. Rolston and M. Tomlinson, *Northern Ireland: Between Civil Rights and Civil War*, London, CSE Books, 1980.
O'Dowd, L. 'Trends and Potential of the Service Sector in Northern Ireland', in P. Teague (ed.), *Beyond the Rhetoric: Politics, the Economy and Social Policy in Northern Ireland*, London: Lawrence and Wishart, 1987, pp. 183-210.
O'Dowd, L. and Rolston, B., 'Bringing Hong Kong to Belfast? The Case of an Enterprise Zone', *International Journal of Urban and Regional Research* 9(1), 1985, 218-232.
O'Dowd, L., Rolston, B. and Tomlinson, M. *Northern Ireland: Between Civil Rights and Civil War*, London: CSE Books, 1980.
Pahl, R., *Divisions of Labour*, Oxford: Basil Blackwell, 1984.
Pahl, R. and Wilson, P., *Industry and Training on the Isle of Sheppey in the 1980s*, Work Strategies Unit, University of Kent, 1986.

Public Inquiry into Unemployment: Report, Belfast: Springhill Community House, 1983.

Quigley Report, Economic and Industrial Strategy for Northern Ireland: Report of a Review Team, Belfast 1976.

Rea, D., (ed.) *Political Co-operation in Divided Societies*, Dublin: Gill and Macmillan, 1983.

Regional Trends, London: H.M.S.O., 1987.

Rowthorn, B., 'Northern Ireland: An Economy in Crisis', in Teague, P., (ed) *Beyond the Rhetoric: Politics, the Economy and Social Policy in Northern Ireland*, London: Lawrence and Wishart, 1987, pp. 111-135.

Rowthorn, B., 'Unemployment: the Widening Sectarian Gap', *Fortnight* 16/12/85, pp. 4-5.

Royal Group of Hospitals Unit of Management, *Ideas for Savings—Financial Year 1988/9.*

Shearman, H., 'Conflict in Northern Ireland', in *The Year Book of World Affairs 1982.*

Smith, A. (Chairperson), *The Nation's Health*, London: King Edward's Hospital Fund for London, 1988.

Smith, D. *Equality and Inequality in Northern Ireland: Part One, Employment and Unemployment*, London: Policy Studies Institute, 1987.

Smith, D. *Equality and Inequality in Northern Ireland: Part Three, Perceptions and Views*, London: Policy Studies Institute, 1987.

Smith, R., *Unemployment and Health: A Disaster and a Challenge*, Oxford: Oxford University Press, 1987.

Standing Advisory Commission on Human Rights, *Religious and Political Discrimination and Equality of Opportunity in Northern Ireland: Report on Fair Employment*, London: H.M.S.O., Cm. 237, 1987.

Stitt, S., 'A Meagre, Cheap and Usually Unhealthy Diet', *Scope* No. 103, May, 1987, pp. 10-12.

Sunday Times.

Teague, P., (ed) *Beyond the Rhetoric: Politics, the Economy and Social Policy in Northern Ireland*, London: Lawrence and Wishart, 1987.

Therborn, G., *Why Some Peoples are more Unemployed than Others: The Strange Paradox of Growth and Unemployment*, London: Verso, 1986.

Tomlinson, M., 'Relegating Local Government', in L. O'Dowd, B. Rolston, and M. Tomlinson, *Northern Ireland: Between Civil Rights and Civil War*, London: CSE Books, 1980.

Trew, K. and Kilpatrick, R., *The Daily Life of the Unemployed*, Belfast: Queen's University, 1984.

Trewsdale, J., *Unemployment in Northern Ireland, 1974-1979*, Belfast: Northern Ireland Economic Council, 1980.

Trewsdale, J., *The aftermath of recession: Changing patterns in female employment and unemployment in Northern Ireland*, Belfast: Equal Opportunities Commission, 1987.

Ulster.
Ulster Business.
Unemployment Bulletin.
Unemployment: Recommendations for Action Within a Strategy for Economic Development, Belfast 1982.
West Belfast: Some of the Facts behind the Issues, Falls Community Council, 1987.
Whitehead, M., *The Health Divide: Inequalities in Health in the 1980s*, London, Health Education Council, 1987.
Wiener, R., *The Rape and Plunder of the Shankill*, Belfast: Farset Press, 1980.
Wilson, D. and Kearney, O., *West Belfast—The Way Forward?*, 1988.